Anyone *Can* Papercraft

A STEP-BY-STEP GUIDE TO ESSENTIAL PAPER SKILLS

Elizabeth Moad

ARCTURUS

ARCTURUS

This edition published in 2014 by Arcturus Publishing Limited
26/27 Bickels Yard, 151–153 Bermondsey Street,
London SE1 3HA

ISBN: 978-1-78404-049-9
AD004132UK

Printed in China

CONTENTS

INTRODUCTION · · · · · · · · · · · · · · · · · · · **6**
   Choosing Paper · · · · · · · · · · · · · · · · · · · 8
   Basic Tool Kit · · · · · · · · · · · · · · · · · · · 12
   Basic Techniques · · · · · · · · · · · · · · · · · · · 14

CARDS, TAGS AND WRAPPING · · · · · · · · · · · · **18**
   Flower Power · · · · · · · · · · · · · · · · · · · 20
   Concertina Card · · · · · · · · · · · · · · · · · · · 22
   Gift Bow · · · · · · · · · · · · · · · · · · · 24
   Quilled Butterfly · · · · · · · · · · · · · · · · · · · 26
   Punched Tags · · · · · · · · · · · · · · · · · · · 28
   Small Gift Bag · · · · · · · · · · · · · · · · · · · 30
   Owl Gift Tags · · · · · · · · · · · · · · · · · · · 32
   Wedding Favour Box · · · · · · · · · · · · · · · · · · · 34
   Rubber Stamped Envelope and Notelets · · · · · · · · · · 38
   New-Home Pop-Up Card · · · · · · · · · · · · · · · · · · · 40
   Kirigami Card · · · · · · · · · · · · · · · · · · · 42
   Good-Luck Box · · · · · · · · · · · · · · · · · · · 44
   Woven Heart Tag · · · · · · · · · · · · · · · · · · · 48

KEEPSAKES AND GIFTS · · · · · · · · · · · · · · · **50**
   Stitched Flower Collage · · · · · · · · · · · · · · · · · · · 52
   Note Block with Roses · · · · · · · · · · · · · · · · · · · 56
   Book Cover with Birds · · · · · · · · · · · · · · · · · · · 60
   Paper Bead Necklace · · · · · · · · · · · · · · · · · · · 62
   Scottie Dog Note-Holder · · · · · · · · · · · · · · · · · · · 66
   Quilled Picture · · · · · · · · · · · · · · · · · · · 68
   Posy of Poppies · · · · · · · · · · · · · · · · · · · 72
   Stencilled Pencil Pot and Note Holder · · · · · · · · · · · 76
   Folded Paper Picture · · · · · · · · · · · · · · · · · · · 78

HOLIDAYS AND SPECIAL OCCASIONS · · · · · · **82**
   Christmas Garlands · · · · · · · · · · · · · · · · · · · 84
   Fringed Frilly Flower Picture · · · · · · · · · · · · · · · · 88
   Baby Bunting · · · · · · · · · · · · · · · · · · · 92
   Leopard-Print Style · · · · · · · · · · · · · · · · · · · 96
   Pompom Tissue Flower Heart · · · · · · · · · · · · · · · · 100
   Woven Star Christmas Decorations · · · · · · · · · · · · · 102
   Halloween Decoration · · · · · · · · · · · · · · · · · · · 108
   Christmas Poinsettia Wreath · · · · · · · · · · · · · · · · 112

TEMPLATES · · · · · · · · · · · · · · · · · · · **116**

INTRODUCTION

Even in this ultra high-tech age of gadgets and gizmos, we still rely on paper in our day-to-day lives. It is everywhere, in newspapers, packaging, gift wrap, books and of course art materials, so there are no shortages when it comes to crafting! A personally handmade gift means much more to both giver and recipient than one that has been bought from a shop, and with a few easy techniques it's possible to make a card, gift or decoration that is not only unique, but professional and eye-catching.

The wonderful aspect of papercrafting that has enthralled me for more than ten years is that it is so versatile. The unassuming nature of paper means that it is often thrown away without consideration, but with careful folding, snipping, colouring or curling you can make really pretty items such as cards, tags, bunting or even pictures to be proud of. The equally wonderful feature of paper is that it costs very little, so if you make mistakes you can just start again without worrying about the expense. This applies to beginners and more experienced crafters too, as none of us always gets things right first time!

There is a wide range of papers available in various colours, patterns and textures. As you too become entranced with this craft you will become familiar with which types of paper work well for your purpose, then your stock of paper will grow so that you have plenty on hand to choose for your projects. You will also find it hard to put paper into recycling bins as ideas will come to you for using it in projects! Papercrafters tend to become hoarders, you will find.

This book is an introduction to the world of papercrafts, with projects illustrating various techniques such as punching, stamping, quilling and stitching with paper. However, this is just a launch pad from which you can go on to apply the skills you have learnt to further projects, exploring your creativity.

ABOUT PAPER

One of the earliest forms of paper was developed by the Ancient Egyptians from the papyrus plant, from which the word 'paper' derives. The technique of papermaking spread across the world but remained an artisan activity until the Industrial Revolution, when the first machine for making paper was patented in 1798. Machine-made papers are those that we encounter in everyday life, with the fibres lying in one direction (the grain).

With the coming of computer technology there has been a move to reduce the use of paper in order to conserve forests and help the environment. This is a good policy, though paper manufacturers are generally ecologically aware and the paper industry contributes to sustainable forest management. Papercrafters are also doing their bit for the environment, as we see value where others see waste. Old books, used gift wrap, out-of-date maps and so forth can all be put to good use and some examples are shown in the projects. I hope that by creating the projects in this book you will not only begin to love paper, but also view it in an entirely different way!

HOW TO USE THIS BOOK

If you are a complete beginner to papercrafts it is a good idea to start by familiarizing yourself with the tools and papers needed (pp. 8–13) before turning to the projects. These are divided into three sections for easy reference. The first, beginning with cards, tags and wrapping projects, is an introduction to the essential techniques of papercraft without the necessity for a lot of new and expensive tools. Then, moving on to keepsakes and gifts, the basic techniques are developed further to make more long-lasting items such as pictures, jewellery and stationery. Finally, in the section on holidays and special occasions, you will discover how to make paper decorations such as garlands and bunting. However, you do not have to follow the book from start to finish – you can dip in to each chapter and out again as you wish.

CHOOSING PAPER

There is such an array of papers and card available that the choice of colours, patterns, themes, textures and weights can be bewildering at first. Specialist handmade papers can be purchased in craft shops and it is a pleasure when on holiday to find new sources of papers. However, these papers can be so treasured that they are saved and never used!

It is important to select the colour and weight of paper most appropriate for the project you are starting, and as you build your craft collection you will have an increasingly large range at home to choose from.

GRAIN

Machine-made paper has a grain which comes from how the fibres of the paper are arranged – typically, parallel to each other across the sheet. Knowing the grain direction is important when tearing a sheet of paper. However, not all paper has a grain; handmade paper has fibres that lie in all directions.

WEIGHT

The weight of the paper or card intended for a project is important. Strong paper may be too thin for a greetings card, for example, as it won't stand up without curling. In Europe, paper weight is measured in a metric system of grams per square metre, abbreviated to 'gsm' or 'g/m', while in the USA, and formerly in the UK, the measure denotes the weight of a ream (500 sheets) of a given size in pounds. General paper used in office printers and photocopiers is around 80 gsm [20 lb]. A good average weight of card is 260–300 gsm [about 140 lb].

PAPER TYPES

There are many types of paper available, some in everyday use and others more specialist and found in craft shops. Listed here are the various types used in the projects. However, this is not an exhaustive list of what you can find.

PLAIN

With the increased popularity of papercrafting in recent years, there is now a wonderful selection of plain paper and card in all the colours of the rainbow. There is a standard size of 30.5 cm [12 in] square for sheets of card and patterned papers from many craft suppliers. An A4 size is also common in plain colours.

WRAPPING

Also called gift wrap, wrapping paper is generally sold in large sheets or on a roll. The advantages are the strength, variety of patterns and low price.

PRINTED PATTERNS

The range of printed papers available is fantastic and gives crafters an amazing source of single-sided and often double-sided paper and card. Those that are printed on both sides are ideal for making decorations.

UPCYCLED

Household papers such as magazines, old books, music sheets, wrapping papers and old maps are a great source for crafting. These papers are often lightweight and can be rolled or curled easily. Note that very old papers may be fragile.

MULBERRY

This paper is made from the mulberry tree, using the inner fibres to create a texture throughout. The main characteristic is the random fibre pattern which means it has no grain, but makes it remarkably durable. Its unique texture makes it good for collage and projects that can display the texture.

CRÊPE

This is tissue paper that has been coated with size (a glue-like substance) and then creased to make slight gathers. One of the lightest papers, it is normally less than 35 gsm [10lb]. Crêpe paper has some stretch and is quite robust, which is why it is ideal for making flowers, such as the poppies on p. 72.

TISSUE

The lightest of all papers, tissue paper is mainly used for gift-wrapping presents to protect delicate items and to make the presentation more special. It comes in many colours, sometimes with a pattern. It can be used for découpage, collage and a range of other projects, including the pompom flowers on p. 100.

PAPER STORAGE

Many crafters don't have a lot of space for storing their paper. If you can, separate your papers into categories and store flat, without stacking, or the lower papers will be crushed. Paper fades in direct sunlight, so store away from windows and other areas that are sunlit.

CARD

Card or 'cardstock' as it is often referred to, has seen a dramatic increase in colour range over recent years. Previously the colour palette of card was very limited with just one or two shades of the seven rainbow colours. Now crafters have an amazing choice of a whole spectrum of colour ranges, with many shades of every colour, which allows for the layering or 'matting' as it is called of several pieces differing in sizes, of harmonious colours for a background. Card has also been developed with an inner 'core' contrast colour which can be exposed through sanding or tearing. Textured card is also very popular with a 'linen' effect, or embossed patterns creating a raised aspect to the card.

Cardstock comes in a variety of sizes for paper crafting and cardmaking, but is most commonly found in 12inch x 12inch squares.

BASIC TOOL KIT

The good news is that papercrafting does not require a huge array of tools. While some specialist tools are used in the projects, it is best at first to purchase just the essentials described here and then build up your kit gradually over time.

1. COCKTAIL STICKS

Cocktail sticks, or toothpicks, are used to apply small dots of glue to papers. Alternatively, you can use a needle tool or a fine-tip applicator which is a metal tip attached to a glue pot, with a very narrow hole that allows you to apply just a tiny spot of glue straight from the pot.

2. CUTTING MAT

A self-healing cutting mat is essential. When it is cut with a knife, the edges of the cut come together again, leaving no indent. However, the mat can only cope with vertical cuts; angled cuts will gouge out the material. The grid marked on the mat can be used as guides for cutting to save time measuring. Mats are not only useful when cutting papers with a craft knife – they also protect your work surface from glue and scissors.

3. DOUBLE-SIDED TAPE

This is narrow tape which is adhesive on both sides, used for mounting paper or card.

4. FOAM PADS

Adhesive foam pads come in all shapes and sizes and are great for achieving a raised effect when attaching items. Foam pads are adhesive on both sides – simply remove the backing paper and stick them to your card or paper.

5. PENCIL AND ERASER

An HB pencil and an eraser are required for marking lines on graph paper and for tracing templates.

6. METAL RULER

A metal ruler is needed when cutting with a craft knife. A ruler with a cork base to stop it from slipping is best.

7. CRAFT KNIFE

For cutting straight edges you will need a craft knife, which should always be used on a cutting mat with a metal ruler. Change the blade regularly so that it is always sharp.

8. SCISSORS

A pair of small, fine-pointed scissors is essential to papercrafting so that you can cut small and delicate areas. Larger scissors are sometimes needed to cut through many layers, such as a tissue pompom project.

9. NEEDLE TOOL

A needle tool is a metal point on a handle which is useful for rolling paper around, leaving a hole in the centre. The needle part is used to make holes for brads and some crafters also like to apply glue with it rather than a cocktail stick.

10. TWEEZERS

A pair of fine-tipped tweezers are necessary for picking up and positioning tiny items such as wiggly eyes. Some tweezers are self-locking so that you do not need to keep them squeezed.

11. GLUE STICK AND PVA (WHITE) GLUE

Regular PVA glue is fine but it should not be very runny, since too much water in glue makes the papers too wet. A tacky PVA is best, but you can use a water-based non-toxic glue as long as it dries clear.

12. STRONG GLUE

(Superglue TM) is extremely powerful glue that is concentrated in to small units, so little is required. Once an item is attached with strong glue it dries very quickly and cannot be repositioned. Care should be taken when using strong glue not to get it on your hands.

BASIC TECHNIQUES

It is important in papercrafts to use the right tool for the job in order to achieve a professional finish. While a handmade effect is of course desirable, uneven cutting or a wonky edge can really stand out, spoiling the finished item. Here some basic techniques are demonstrated to enable you to get it right first time.

CUTTING

When you are cutting large sheets of paper or card you will only be able to achieve a straight line by using a craft knife and ruler, or a guillotine; I find that a knife and ruler are much more versatile and give more cutting options. Place the paper on a self-healing cutting mat. You can use the grid lines on the mat as cutting guides rather than marking with pencil where you want to cut. Place the ruler on the paper and hold in place with one hand. With the other hand, place the craft knife against the ruler, press down and pull towards you. When cutting large sheets, I find it easier to stand up.

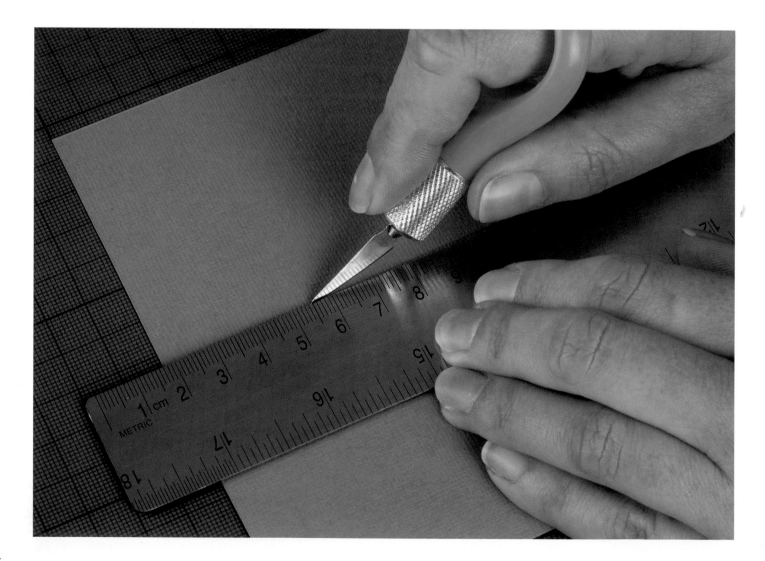

GLUEING

PVA (white) glue is needed for joining paper, card and some embellishments, but it is not used over large areas or the paper will cockle (crinkle) from its wetness. Here double-sided tape is used instead.

I have found that applying PVA glue with a cocktail stick (or toothpick) is the best method. The fine point allows exact positioning and more control over where the glue goes. I tend to put a small amount of glue on to kitchen foil so that the pot of glue is not always open and drying out.

A glue stick is a useful way of applying glue to medium-sized areas. The glue is less runny than PVA glue and some crafters are more comfortable using it. The sticks of glue do tend to dry out quickly, so put the cap back on immediately after use.

POSITIONING

Many crafters struggle with positioning elements correctly. Using double-sided tape, following the technique below, allows you to reposition the paper or card if needed, then stick it down exactly where you want.

Begin by placing lengths of narrow double-sided tape on all four edges of the paper. Detach the end of the backing paper of one length, pull it off to the halfway point, then press to crease. Do this for all four strips. You will then have four pieces of backing paper sticking out from the four sides. Position the paper where you need it and when you are happy it is in the right place, pull out each of the protruding ends of the backing paper and press the paper down.

SCORING AND FOLDING

You will find that scoring paper allows it to be folded neatly and easily. A crisper fold is created and results in a more professional finish. Place the ruler on the paper or card where you need the fold and draw the tool along the ruler, pressing down all the time. Use both hands to fold the paper or card along the score line. Once it is folded, use a bone folder held horizontally to carefully flatten the crease. If you don't have a bone folder, the back of a teaspoon will do the job.

Cards, tags and wrapping

Although our access to email and the internet is a huge benefit in the modern world, an e-card to an inbox is just not as nice as a handmade card arriving through the letterbox. Papercrafting has a natural affinity to making greeting cards and all sorts of gift wrap and allows you to tailor them to the recipient, while making your own bags and boxes allows you to determine the size, shape, colour and finishing touches, rather than settling for mass-produced standard sizes. You will soon discover that presenting something you have made yourself will never fail to give pleasure.

FLOWER POWER

Papercrafting at its simplest just needs paper, scissors and glue. By using fresh, coordinating bright colours, you can create stylish flowers for a modern greeting card. Templates are provided for this project, but as you gain confidence, experiment with varying the sizes and shapes of the petals and leaves to make your own unique designs. As flowers have a universal appeal, they are suitable for many occasions and this design can be adapted for birthdays, Mother's Day, or get-well cards by adding a greeting if you wish.

You will need

- Pink paper in three shades, each 10 x 5 cm [4 x 2 in]
- Purple paper, 5 x 2.5 cm [2 x 1 in]
- Turquoise paper, 13 x 13 cm [5¼ x 5¼ in]
- Light blue card, 12 x 13 cm [4¾ x 5¼ in]
- Pink card blank, 12.5 x 18 cm [5 x 7 in]
- White glue
- Light pink felt pen
- Ribbon

Felt pens have been used to colour the tips of the petals here, but this can be omitted.

1 ◁ Use the templates on p. 127 to cut five petals from bright pink paper. Now repeat using two more shades of coordinating pink paper. Cut out three central discs for the flowers from purple paper, using the template. Glue the light blue card on to the pink card.

2 ▷ Lightly colour the tip of each petal on one side with felt pen. Colour the central discs on the top only. Colouring the top of the central disc and flower tips makes them less uniform and 'flat'. Using white glue and a cocktail stick (toothpick), apply glue to the back of the central discs and glue the petals on.

3 ▷ Now cut a narrow stalk from turquoise paper and glue this to the light blue card. Glue a flower to the top of the stalk. Cut three leaves from turquoise paper and colour the edges with the pink felt pen. Assemble the stalks, leaves and flowers as shown then glue in place.

For a quick gift tag to match, make just one flower and mount with a short stalk on a light blue circle of card, diameter 7.5 cm [3 in]. Then mount this on to a pink card 9 cm [3½ in] in diameter. Thread ribbon through a hole in the circle top.

CONCERTINA CARD

An economical and environmentally friendly way of papercrafting is to upcycle papers that would generally be discarded. In this project, a novel heading for the recycling pile was rescued to use the pages for a concertina shape. Any book is suitable as their pages are an ideal weight for folding, neither too thick nor too thin. Aged paper can be frail, so if you are using a book that has been on your shelves for a long while it is best to test a page for folding purposes first. In this project the blank margin of the page is used.

You will need

- Basic tool kit
- Three strips from an old book, each 16 x 5 cm [6¼ x 2 in]
- Orange card, 11.5 cm [4½ in] square
- Orange gemstones, 5 mm [³⁄₁₆ in]
- Brown card blank, 13 cm [5¼ in] square

1 ▷ Cut three strips of paper 5 cm [2 in] wide and 16 cm [6¼ in] long, including part of the blank margin of the pages. Concertina the strip by folding over the short edge at 1 cm [⅜ in] intervals. Continue folding to the end and repeat with the other two lengths.

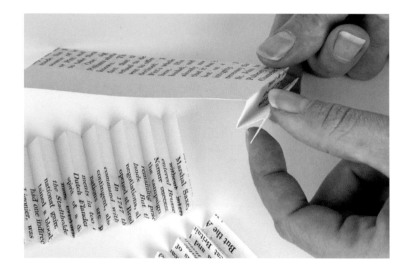

2 ▽ Using small scissors, snip the ends of the concertina folds at the blank margin on all three strips to make points.

3 ▷ Glue the three lengths together using white glue, applying it with a cocktail stick (toothpick). Then join the two ends together to form a circle.

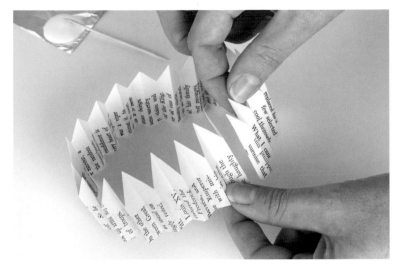

4 ◁ Place a generous amount of glue on the centre of the orange card and press the concertina ring on top of the glue, with the points outwards. Hold for several seconds for the glue to dry or the concertina will spring up. Mount the orange card to the brown card using double-sided tape, then apply an orange gemstone to the centre of the concertina circle and one to each corner of the orange card. If the gemstones are not self-adhesive, use strong glue.

When sending cards with a three-dimensional feature such as this concertina card, place them in a small box so that they are not flattened while in transit.

GIFT BOW

A gift bow adds a special touch to a gift box or parcel, and when it is a homemade bow it becomes super special! Wrapping paper is ideal for making bows as it twists and turns easily for the loops needed in the construction of the bow. It also has the advantage that the bow can be coordinated with the gift wrap on the parcel. You can use paper that is patterned on both sides, though paper that is plain on one side, as shown here, makes for an equally effective bow.

You will need

• Basic tool kit
• Wrapping paper, 14 x 20 cm [5½ x 7¾ in]

1 ▽ Using scissors or a craft knife and cutting mat, cut strips of paper 13 mm [½ in] wide in lengths as follows; four strips 20 cm [7¾ in], three 16 cm [6¼ in], two 14 cm [5½ in], one 12 cm [4¾ in] and one 6 cm [2⅜ in].

2 ▽ Take one of the 20 cm [7¾ in] strips and loop and twist one end of the paper around so the tip reaches the centre of the strip. Glue in place with white glue applied with a cocktail stick (toothpick).

3 ▽ Loop the other end of the strip and twist it round to the centre so it meets the end already glued in step 1. Glue it in place.

If you use shiny gift wrap, hold the glued parts for several seconds as the glue will take slightly longer to set. You can double the dimensions of the paper strips to make an even larger bow.

4 ◁ Repeat this looping and twisting with all the other strips except the shortest length. Once looped, keep them arranged in order of sizes. Make the shortest length into a ring by glueing it end to end – this will be the final centrepiece to the bow.

5 ◁ Take the four largest looped shapes and glue the centres together so they form a circle. Glue the three looped shapes of the next size together to make another circle. Glue the two loops made with 14 cm [5½ in] lengths together, forming a cross shape.

6 ▷ Now glue the small circle into the larger circle. Glue the cross shape into the smaller circle, and glue the smallest looped shape into the cross. Finally, add a loop to the centre of the rosette to finish it.

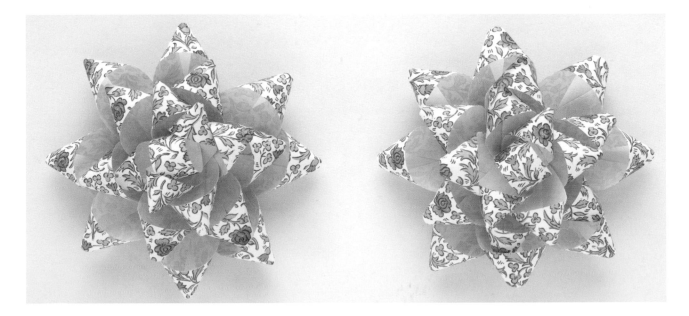

QUILLED BUTTERFLY

Paper quilling is the craft of coiling, rolling and pinching strips of paper. It is a historic craft that dates back many centuries but is still very popular today because of the unique shapes that can be made. You can use a quilling tool for this butterfly if you have one, but here the paper is rolled around a needle tool to form swirly scrolls. In order to make identical rings, the paper is wrapped around a piece of wooden dowel. If you don't have dowel, you can improvise with items such as lids of glue pots, ends of wooden spoons, or anything else round and smooth that you can slide paper off.

You will need

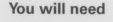

- Basic tool kit
- Needle tool or quilling tool
- Wooden dowel in two sizes, 25 mm [1 in] and 15 mm [⅝ in] diameter
- Papers, 3 mm [⅛ in] wide, in brown, red and pink
- Green card, 10 x 15 cm [4 x 6 in]
- Pink card, 12 x 18 cm [4¾ x 7 in]
- Red card blank 13 x 19 cm [5¼ x 7½ in]

1 ◁ Take a 25 cm [10 in] length of red paper and wrap it around a piece of wooden dowel 15 mm [⅝ in] in diameter. Wrap around three times and glue the end in place, then slide the paper ring off the dowel. Repeat five times, creating the larger wings. Then, using a 15 cm [6 in] length of the red paper, make rings in the same way using the 25 mm [1 in] wooden dowel. Pinch all the rings lightly to make eye shapes.

2 ▷ Take a 20 cm [7¾ in] length of pink paper and roll one end around a needle tool. Continue rolling until you reach 5 cm [2 in] before the other end, then remove the needle tool, turn the paper over, and roll the other end towards the first coil, creating an S-shaped scroll. Make five more, then make six in the same way using 15 cm [6 in] lengths.

3 ◁ Cut a 10 cm [4 in] strip of the brown paper, fold in half and glue for 1 cm [⅜ in] from the fold, leaving the ends free. Glue this to the green card with two large and two small wings, then insert the scrolls into the wing shapes. Make three butterflies in this way and mount the card to pink card then the red card blank.

Butterfly Gift Tag

For the matching tag cut one tag shape from red card and one slightly smaller from coral coloured card. Mount together, punch a hole and thread red and orange ribbon through. Attach a rectangle of green card and then make a butterfly as per the instructions for the main card.

You can cut your own paper strips for quilling or they can be purchased ready-cut in many shades and widths. If you don't have a needle tool, you can roll strips around a cocktail stick (toothpick).

PUNCHED TAGS

Paper punches come in various shapes and sizes, but all are based on the principles of the good old-fashioned office hole punch; paper or card is inserted in the shaped punch, the punch is pressed down and the shape is cut out. The huge advantage of punches is that little effort is needed to make hundreds of identical shapes. Here a daisy punch is used to make a quick and easy gift tag in bright colours. The centres of the flowers are 'brads' – metal fasteners that have two wings pushed out on the reverse side to keep them in place and secure shapes together. These brads are another favourite for papercrafters.

You will need

- Basic tool kit
- Paper: yellow, 10 cm [4 in] square
- Card: yellow and orange, 13 x 7 cm [5¼ x 2¾ in]
- Ribbon: orange organza, 6 mm [¼ in] wide and 20 cm [7¾ in] long
- Brads: pink, green, size 7 mm [¼ in]
- Daisy punch, 2.5 cm [1 in]
- Needle tool

1 ▷ Insert the yellow paper into the slot of the daisy punch and press the lever down to punch out the shape. Repeat to make six daisy shapes in total.

2 ▷ Glue three daisies on to the orange tag made using the template on p. 124. Press the needle tool through the centre of each daisy and the orange card beneath to make a hole. It is best to place the shapes on a foam mat to avoid the needle pricking your fingers.

3 ◁ Now insert pink brads through the holes at each end and a green one in the centre, spread the wings out on the reverse side and press flat. Using foam pads, mount the orange card to a yellow gift tag cut slightly larger. Thread orange organza ribbon through a hole made at the top of the tag. Make another tag, switching the colours of the brads around as shown.

Punches will become blunt over time. To sharpen them, punch through regular kitchen foil several times.

SMALL GIFT BAG

You don't need rulers or complicated measuring to make small gift bags – they are very easy to make, but look so professional! Using a box as a template around which to fold the paper allows you to choose any size you want rather than being restricted to shop sizes. Any box can be used – a soup packet box was the template for this project – but even a book will do. You can use any strong paper, even wallpaper. These pink bags are ideal for a baby shower or christening gifts.

You will need

- Basic tool kit
- Strong wrapping paper with a pink pattern, 33 x 25 cm [13 x 10 in]
- A box or similar shape, 10 x 13 x 5 cm [4 x 5¼ x 2 in]
- Pink ribbon, 45 cm [18 in]

1 ▽ Take the sheet of paper and fold over one long edge at 10 cm [4 in]. This will become the top of the bag.

2 ▽ Now use the box as a mould, wrapping the paper around it to get the shape. Overlap the two short edges and, using double-sided tape, secure them together.

3 ◁ With the box 3.5 cm [1⅜ in] in from the bottom edge (unfolded edge) of the paper, now press one edge around the box edge and down, as if you were wrapping a present. Press the two sides inwards, again around the box edge, using the box as a guide for the creasing and folding. Finally bring the remaining edge upwards and secure with double-sided tape. The end of the box is now contained inside the folds.

4 ◁ Remove the box template by sliding it out from the paper. Now pinch the sides inwards at the top of the bag, creating a gusset.

5 ◁ Using a small hole punch or a needle tool, make two holes at the top of the bag, large enough to allow the ribbon through. Push the ribbon through each hole, insert the gift and tie the ribbon in a bow.

If you are making large numbers of bags you can fold the bottoms over so that they lie flat for easy storage.

OWL GIFT TAGS

One of the most perennially popular motifs is the owl, which appeals to all ages, making it perfect for cards and tags. This wise owl is jazzed up with modern bright colours and quirky eye shapes. Plain colours are used in this project but it works just as well with patterned papers and card, ideal for using up small leftovers from other projects. Here the heart-shape punch is given another function as feathers – many punched shapes can be adapted like this with a little imagination. These tags could easily become place name cards, with the name written on the bottom of the purple card.

You will need

- Basic tool kit
- Circle punches, sizes 2.5 cm [1 in] and 1 cm [⅜ in]
- Heart-shape punch, 2.5 cm [1 in]
- Paper: white, black, yellow, blue, brown, 13 x 10 cm [5¼ x 4 in]
- Card: purple, turquoise and green, 13 x 10 cm [5¼ x 4 in]

1 ▽ Use the template on p. 117 to cut out the owl shape from scrap card such as a cereal box. Then trace round this owl template on to turquoise card and cut out.

If you do not have circle punches, use a computer to print eyes and cut them out.

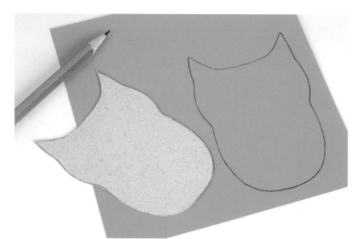

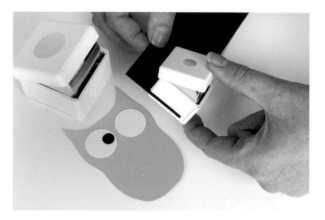

2 △ Using the 2.5 cm [1 in] circle punch and white paper, punch two circles. Use the smaller circle punch to make 1 cm [⅜ in] circles from black paper. Glue the black circles to the white and then on to the owl head, using white glue and a cocktail stick (toothpick).

3 ◁ Using the templates, cut two wings from green card and attach to each side of the owl. Cut a small triangle from yellow paper for a beak and glue between the eyes.

4 ▷ With the heart-shape punch, make 14 heart shapes from blue paper. Glue a row of three hearts, points upwards, to the owl's body. Then glue a row of four hearts on top of the first, then a third row of three hearts to resemble the layers of feathers. For the final layer trim the heart shapes by rounding off the point, then glue these to the owl body.

5 ◁ Turn the owl over so it is face down. Punch two more hearts from brown paper and glue to the bottom of the owl, so just the curved parts overlap the edge – when it is turned over these become the claws. Finally, attach the owl to purple card.

Variation

The owls can be made from traditional browns for perhaps a graduation card, or alternatively from purples which are a great way to use left over paper scraps from other projects.

WEDDING FAVOUR BOX

Mini boxes make great holders for wedding favours, easily holding sugared almonds or other favourites. This pyramid-shaped box is more simple to make than it looks, and with no glueing involved it is constructed in no time. After easy cutting and scoring, all you need to do is fold the sides inwards and then tie them together at the top with ribbon. By making your own wedding favours you can choose the colour scheme and perhaps involve friends and family in the creative process.

1 Copy the template on p. 119 on to scrap card, cut out and transfer on to mauve card. If you are a beginner it is advisable to mark the score lines on the mauve card in pencil as dashed lines, but once you have made several boxes you won't need to do this any more.

You will need

- Basic tool kit
- Purple card, 15 cm [6 in] square
- Dark purple card, 5 cm [2 in] square
- Mauve ribbon, 30 cm [12 in] length
- Heart punch, 2.5 cm [1 in]
- Tiny circle punch or needle tool

To make larger pyramid boxes, enlarge the box template on a photocopier.

2 △ With scissors or a craft knife and cutting mat, cut out the shape where indicated, making sure the corners are neat. For the best results use a craft knife and metal ruler, with the ruler always placed on the good card and the knife cutting into the scrap area.

3 ▽ With a scoring tool and ruler, score lines on all the triangle flaps and the square base as indicated by the dashed lines. Scoring is essential in boxes to allow neat folds and edges.

4 ▷ Fold all the triangle flaps inwards along the score lines. Now use a tiny circle punch to make a hole in the top of each triangle flap. If you don't have a circle punch, use a needle tool.

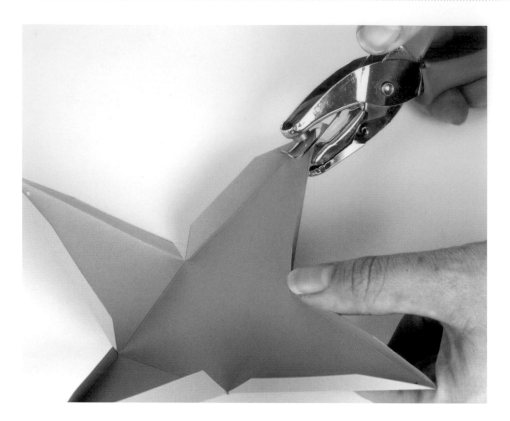

5 ▽ Assemble the box by pushing up the sides, keeping the sides of each triangle folded inwards. Thread ribbon through the four holes and tie in a bow.

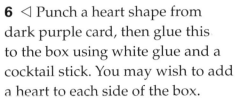

6 ◁ Punch a heart shape from dark purple card, then glue this to the box using white glue and a cocktail stick. You may wish to add a heart to each side of the box.

RUBBER-STAMPED ENVELOPE AND NOTELETS

Rubber stamping is a very popular papercraft and one that is easy to master with a few basic tools. With an acrylic stamp such as the grasses used in this project, an identical image can be printed many times quickly and easily. Inks come in an array of colours, allowing the stamp to be used in many different ways. For a personal touch, an envelope can be made from an A4 sheet of paper and matching notelets stamped for a unique letter.

A flower or butterfly stamp would work well instead of grasses.

You will need

- Basic tool kit
- Rubber stamps – grass stems
- Acrylic block
- Inks: burgundy, green, turquoise
- Cream paper, A4, 100 gsm [68 lb]
- Corner rounder punch
- Glue stick
- Paper towel

1 ▷ Using the template on p. 125, cut out the envelope shape from the cream paper. Score lines where indicated on the template.

2 ◁ Use a corner rounder punch to trim the four outer corners of the envelope shape. Fold the side tabs inwards and, with glue stick, apply a coat of glue along the tabs. Fold the bottom edge up and press down over the tabs. Hold for a few seconds, then turn the envelope over.

3 ▷ The stamp itself is a thin floppy piece of clear rubber that cannot be used on its own, so it needs to be placed on an acrylic block to use. Place the grass stamp on a clear acrylic block – it will stick to the block by itself. Ink the stamp with burgundy ink by holding the block in one hand and lightly dabbing the ink onto the stamp. Ensure that the whole stamp image is covered with a layer of ink.

4 ◁ Press the block, image down, on to the cream envelope. Press firmly then lift off directly upwards to avoid smudges. Clean the stamp with damp paper towel. Place another grass stamp on to an acrylic block and ink with green, then print the image next to the burgundy print. Repeat. Clean the stamp, ink with turquoise and print again.

Matching notelets
Cut an A4 sheet of cream paper in half, then fold each half. Ink the grass stamp with burgundy ink and print on to each folded sheet.

NEW-HOME POP-UP CARD

Pop-up cards are not only fun to receive but great to make as well. There are many techniques and styles of pop-up, as this is a skilled craft in its own right. Here a straightforward technique is used to make a new-home card. Two house shapes are cut into the blue card, then the tops are glued together. The card lies flat when shut but the house is pulled up when the card is opened.

You will need

- Basic tool kit
- Blue card, 14 x 28.5 cm [5½ x 11¼ in]
- Green card, 15 x 30 cm [6 x 11¾ in]

The house shape can be styled and personalized to suit the person receiving the card, such as changing the colour or adding a house number to the door.

1 ◁ Score both pieces of card in half across the width. Use the house template on p. 116 and copy on to the blue card.

2 ◁ Place the card on a cutting mat. With a craft knife and ruler, cut out the lines as indicated on the template. Next, with a scoring tool and ruler, score lines across the base of each house and round the door frame. Attach double-sided tape to the outer edge of the blue card and secure to the green card, ensuring the central score lines match up.

3 △ With the card open, pull up both house shapes to the centre, apply white glue to just the roof part of the houses, then press both houses together. Close the card to make sure everything lies flat once the card is fully closed.

KIRIGAMI CARD

Kirigami (a Japanese word meaning to cut paper) is a version of origami. It starts with a single folded sheet of paper that is cut through the folded layers, then opened out and flattened to reveal the symmetrical shape. It is commonly used for making paper snowflakes and decorations, but here bright blue paper is used with this technique to make a striking card.

You will need

- Basic tool kit
- Blue paper, 13 cm [5¼ in] square
- Cream card blank, 12.5 cm [5 in] square

1 ◁ Take the square of paper and fold in half corner to corner, creating a triangle. Crease the fold with a bone folder, and then fold again corner to corner, forming a smaller triangle. Crease the fold then fold for a third time, creating a small triangle. You will have folds along two sides measuring 9 cm [3½ in] and 6.5 cm [2½ in] and on the third side the folds are open at the top.

2 ▷ Copy the template from p. 117. Line up the folded edges and transfer the design to one side of the triangle, using pencil.

Patterned paper can be used for this technique, but it is best to test first how the pattern works with the design.

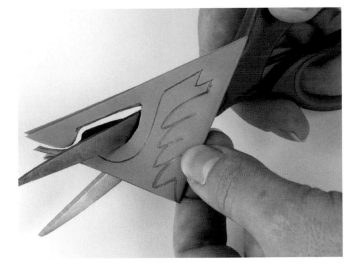

3 ▷ With scissors, cut along the pencil lines drawn. As there are several layers of paper, cutting will require a lot of pressure. Small scissors are used here, but you might find larger scissors have more leverage.

4 ◁ Open out the folded paper to reveal the symmetrical design. At this point you may see edges that have not been cut neatly, in which case you can go in with small scissors to trim them. Apply a light layer of white glue to the paper and secure to the cream card blank.

GOOD-LUCK BOX

Cat-lovers appreciate anything given to them with a feline on, so a box containing a gift and a cat is a double win! The folklore surrounding black cats varies between cultures, with many believing they are good luck and giving them as tokens for major events such as exams, new jobs and even weddings. To avoid fiddly cutting of a lid for the box, the lid is incorporated in the box design so there is only one piece of card to cut. The box lid just slots in, keeping it easy to make and giving a neat finish. Here the cat is made from black card, with moving wiggly eyes for fun and a curly tail using paper quilling for extra effect. This would be great for Halloween treats and tricks.

You will need

- Basic tool kit
- Green card, 30 cm [12 in] square
- Black paper, 5 x 7.5 cm [2 x 3 in]
- Black quilling paper, 3 mm [⅛ in] wide
- Wiggly eyes, 3 mm [⅛ in]
- White felt pen
- Pink felt pen
- Strong glue

1 Copy the template on p. 118 on to the green card. Cut out the box shape where indicated using a craft knife, metal ruler and cutting mat, then score lines where shown with the scoring tool. Cut a slot for the lid tab where indicated on the template.

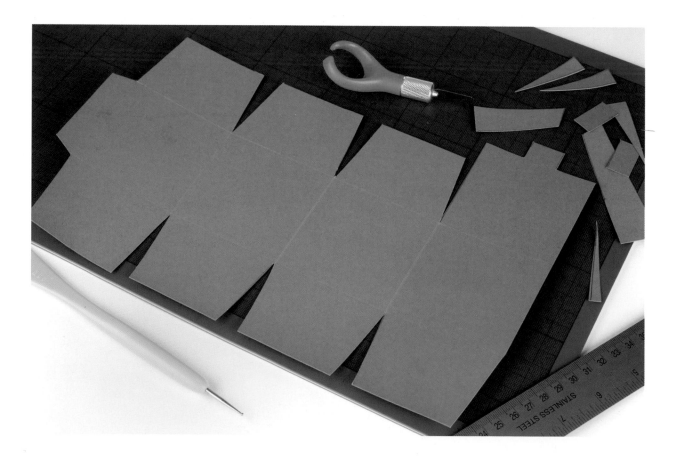

2 ◁ Apply a covering of white glue to the side tab then place this inside the opposite edge of the green card, so the box shape is formed. Hold this or use pegs to keep in place for several seconds while the glue dries. Glueing time will vary with room temperature.

3 ◁ Next, on the box base, fold the two side flaps inwards. Fold the remaining two flaps on the base inwards and glue in place. Turn to the top and check that the lid tab fits in to the slot made on step 1 so that the box closes neatly.

4 ▷ Using the template on p. 127, draw the cat body, head and ears on to black card with white pencil. Cut out the shapes with small scissors.

If you don't have wiggly eyes you can use white and black pen or even green and black pen to colour the eyes. Colour the white or green first then, when dry, draw a black line for the pupil.

5 △ Now pick up a wiggly eye using tweezers, add a tiny amount of strong glue to the reverse and then place it on the black card. Repeat with the other eye. Use a pink pen to draw a nose, then fringe a 1 cm [⅜ in] length of black paper and attach as whiskers.

6 ▽ Take a 10 cm [4 in] length of black quilling paper and curl one end with a needle tool. Glue the straight end to the cat shape and glue to the box. Tie the box with black ribbon.

Variation

As an alternative to a box you can make a tag from green card with black ribbon threaded through a punched hole. The cat is made using the instructions for the main box. Cats can also be made from other colours such as browns or even pinks for fun bright felines.

WOVEN HEART TAG

Weaving strips of paper is a very simple way of transforming plain paper into something special. By weaving just two strips together you can make a pretty heart that can be a gift tag or a hanging decoration. It is adapted from woven-paper heart bags that are a Christmas tradition in Denmark, where each child receives one filled with sweets. This heart uses red and pink colours for a striking combination, but if they were made for a wedding the colours could be changed to match the overall scheme.

You will need

- Basic tool kit
- Red and pink heavyweight paper or card, 13 x 10 cm [5¼ x 4 in] each
- Ribbon (optional)

1 ◁ Using the template on p. 119, cut one piece from red paper and one from pink. Cut along the centre of each shape where indicated to make a slit.

2 ▷ Take the red piece of paper, lift up one section and slot underneath the corresponding pink section of paper. Weave the strips so that one is up and under each way.

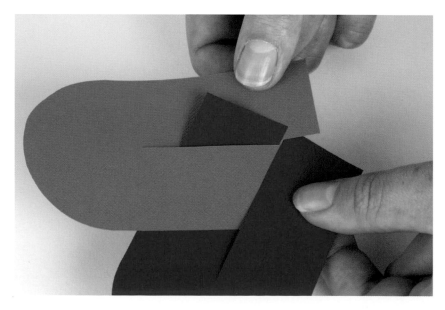

3 ◁ Apply white glue under the end of each section, using a cocktail stick (toothpick). Add ribbon to make a hanging decoration if you wish.

Each shape could be cut into four strips instead of two, then woven for a different pattern.

Keepsakes and gifts

The gifts we send and receive for birthdays, weddings and special occasions are an important part of life, as are those given out of the blue just to say 'I care'. A homemade present is the most personal of all, showing that you have taken the time to create something appealing for a friend or family member. A great advantage of papercrafts is that the gifts and keepsakes shown in these projects are low cost in terms of both materials and equipment. The investment is your time, and through this you tell the recipient how special they are to you.

STITCHED FLOWER COLLAGE

By glueing textured paper to a background then stitching, you can add interesting and varied texture to papercrafts. For quick results, a sewing machine can be used with paper and card, as in this flower project. However, many crafters also enjoy handstitching paper and sewing in embellishments such as buttons or beads. When sewing paper it is essential to tape the ends of the thread on the reverse side as knots will slip through the holes. Mulberry paper is used here for a delicate effect, though its fibres make it strong to use.

1 Cut out four long, thin stems from green mulberry paper. Arrange on the light purple card, overlapping two stems, and glue into place. Use glue stick when attaching fine papers as white glue is too wet for them.

You will need

- Basic tool kit
- Mulberry paper: purple and green, 7.5 x 18 cm [3 x 7 in]
- Card: light purple, 15 x 20 cm [6 x 7¾ in]; dark purple, 20 x 25 cm [7¾ x 10 in]
- Thread: purple and green
- Wiggly eyes, 3 mm [⅛ in]
- Glue stick
- Sewing needle
- Picture frame to fit 20 x 25 cm [7¾ x 10 in]

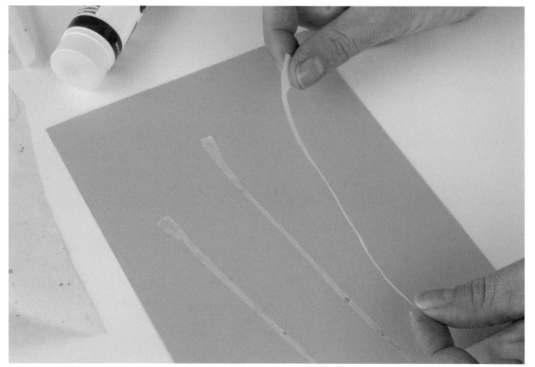

Card and paper will slip beneath the foot of a sewing machine and will feel different from fabric when you are machining, so practise first on scrap paper before beginning the main project.

2 ◁ Thread a sewing machine with green thread and set it to running stitch, medium to large stitch size. Place the card under the foot and carefully insert the needle into the top of the stem. Stitch along all the stems.

3 ▷ Remove the card from the sewing machine. Thread the loose ends of green thread on to a needle and pull through to the reverse side of the card. Tape the ends in place and trim excess thread.

4 △ Take the purple mulberry paper and cut out petal sections to make the carnation flowers. These are randomly cut for the collage effect so it is best to cut several, arrange and overlap them then glue in place.

5 △ Thread the sewing machine with purple thread and, with the same stitch setting, sew at slow speed through the flower, radiating outwards from the top of the stem. Turn the card round then stitch back to the stem top. Do this several times for each flower.

6 ▽ Remove the card from the sewing machine and thread the loose ends of purple thread through to the reverse side of the card as before.

7 Tape over the ends of the threads to hold them in place and trim the excess. Mount to dark purple card and place in a picture frame.

NOTE BLOCK WITH ROSES

Yellow roses are an eternal favourite for many occasions, including weddings and anniversaries. With this easy technique you can make very pretty roses in no time at all to decorate all manner of items for special gifts, such as the note block here. Ordinary office paper is used to make a spiral, the edges are lightly inked with orange, then the paper is coiled inwards with a quilling tool to create the rose. Once this technique is mastered it becomes a favourite of many papercrafters for its simplicity and pretty results.

You will need

- Basic tool kit
- Yellow paper, A4
- Green paper, 5 x 7.5 cm [2 x 3 in]
- Orange inkpad
- Quilling tool
- Noteblock, 8.5 cm [3¼ in] square
- Blue card, 20.5 x 9.5 cm [8 x 3⅛ in]
- Corner rounder punch (optional)

1 ◁ Copy the large and small rose templates on p. 117. Place on yellow paper and use masking tape to hold in place if you wish. With small scissors, roughly cut around the outside of the shapes, cutting through both the yellow and the paper template. Then cut the inner spiral following the template. Discard the template or put aside for future use.

2 ▷ With small scissors, cut around this spiral on the other side to create a wavy edge. It can be irregular, so don't worry too much about keeping the waves symmetrical.

3 ◁ Ink the wavy cut edges with the orange ink pad, lightly dabbing on the edge of the paper. Colour both sides and leave to dry.

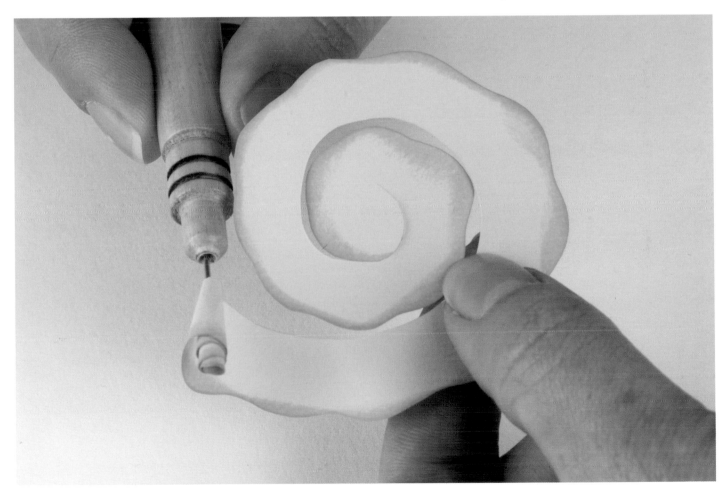

These can be scaled up on a photocopier to make larger roses.

4 △ Using a quilling tool, slot the paper through the prongs and start coiling from the narrow end. Continue to coil the paper by turning the tool around, then remove the tool and let the coil unwind.

5 ▷ Apply glue to the centre of the spiral and then press the coiled part on to the glue. Hold for a few seconds. Repeat to make four large and three small roses.

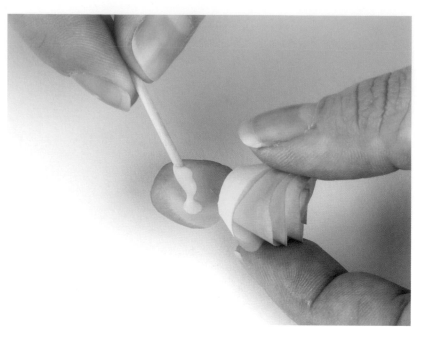

6 ▽ Make the note block cover by scoring at 9 cm [3½ in] and 11.5 cm [4½ in] from one short edge of the blue card. Attach the note block to the blue card at the base and the spine. Glue the roses to the centre of the top cover. Cut four leaves from green paper, using the template on p. 127, crease slightly and glue under the roses.

Variation – Matching tag
Three roses

A tag is made by using a die cutter to make a scalloped edged circle from blue card, a hole punched and narrow orange ribbon threaded through. Three yellow roses are made and attached with three small leaves.

BOOK COVER WITH BIRDS

A plain notebook can be transformed into a gift with just the addition of cute paper birds. One template is enough to cut out multiple bird shapes, with the range of patterned papers here adding variety and colour. Some birds have wings and one cheeky bird faces the other way to the rest for added variation. A brown felt pen provides the beaks and the legs are just drawn with a black pen. This project is a great way to use up leftover pieces of paper from other crafting projects. It could be personalized by cutting initials from paper and glueing these on in place of one bird.

You will need

- Basic tool kit
- Patterned papers of various colours
- Brown felt pen
- Orange inkpad
- Black fine-tip pen
- Kraft notebook, 21 x 15 cm [8¼ x 6 in]

1 ◁ Cut the bird template (p. 127) from scrap card and then draw around it on to the patterned papers. Twelve birds are needed for this size of notebook, so draw and cut out 11 birds facing to the right and, if the paper is only patterned on one side, one bird facing left. Then cut out several wing shapes.

2 ▷ Position the birds on the notebook so they form a grid, three across and four up. Then glue some wings in place beneath one or two birds, and glue all the birds on the notebook. Add the remaining wings to the bodies of some of the birds.

3 ◁ Use the brown pen to colour the beaks of the birds and draw their legs directly on to the notebook with black pen. Here the legs are just made as spindly lines, but you can have fun and draw the legs as if the birds are dancing.

Variation – Matching tag
Two birds

For a matching tag, brown card was cut in to a tag shape, a hole punched and string threaded through. Two birds were cut and made as per the instructions for the notebook. For an alternative these could be love birds if made from red papers.

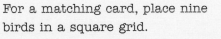

For a matching card, place nine birds in a square grid.

PAPER BEAD NECKLACE

Beads made from paper are great as they are easy to create from material found around the house, such as magazines, books or music sheets. This means that they are eco-friendly and you can produce unique jewellery such as necklaces, bracelets or earrings. To make the beads more durable and waterproof, give them a glaze of varnish or shiny glue. Magazine paper is thin, but you can glue strips end to end for fatter beads; if you use thicker paper, perhaps an old book or poster, then the beads can be formed from shorter lengths. If you need large numbers of one specific colour, use sheets of gift wrap or origami paper.

You will need

- Basic tool kit
- Paper: music sheets
- Diamond Glaze™
- Small paint brush
- Length of thin wire
- Memory wire, 45 cm [18 in]
- Black seed beads
- Round-nose pliers

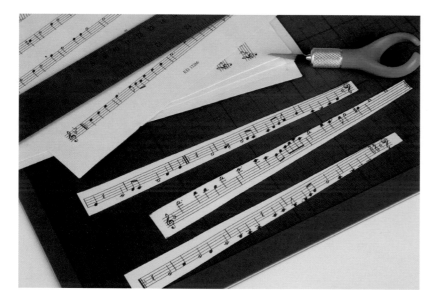

1 ◁ Cut a page of a music sheet to 20 cm [7¾ in] long strips, 1.7 cm [11/16 in] wide at one end and tapering gradually to 1 cm [⅜ in] wide at the other (see the template, p. 119). The widest part will become the length of the tubular bead.

2 ▷ Place the widest end of the strip of paper around a cocktail stick (toothpick). Roll the paper around the stick tightly. Continue to roll, taking care to keep the paper central as it will want to veer off to one side as you roll.

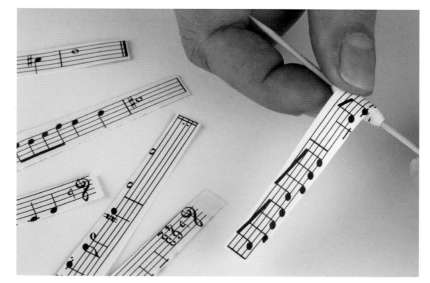

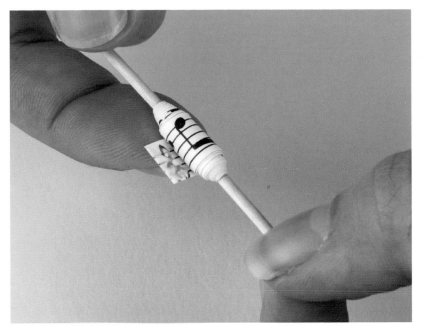

3 ◁ Keep rolling until the end of the paper, then glue the end in place in the middle of the bead.

4 ▽ Remove the cocktail stick (toothpick) by pulling it out from the paper. When you have made several beads of differing sizes, take a brush and cover all the beads with a coat of specialist coating glaze then leave to dry. Here a length of thin floristry wire is used to hold the beads during this process. If the beads are covered with glaze while on the cocktail stick (toothpick) they tend to stick to it and then cannot be removed.

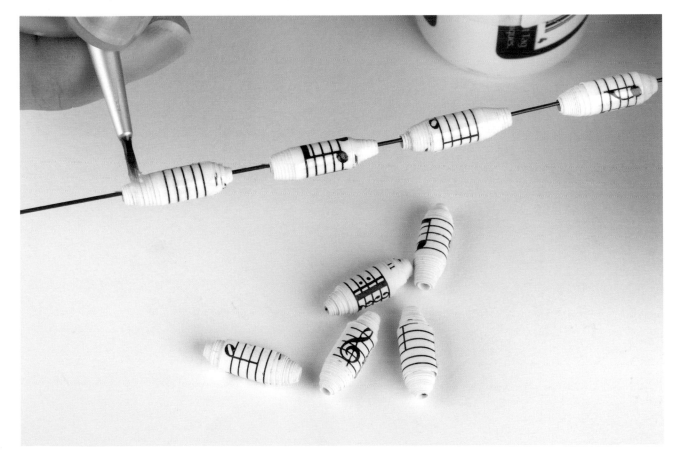

The shape of paper beads depends on the shape of the paper strip. Here long paper strips are used, with the end point finishing at the centre of the bead, but there are many variations and you can experiment with narrower or wider strips.

5 ▷ Thread the beads on to silver memory wire, alternating with small black seed beads to separate them. Continue threading until the wire is full.

6 ▽ With round-nose pliers, curl each end of the memory wire into a loop to stop the beads from falling off. As memory wire always holds its shape, fasteners are not needed as it is stretched to put on, then the wire springs back to hold in place around the neck.

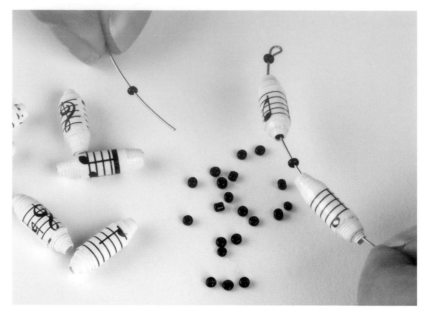

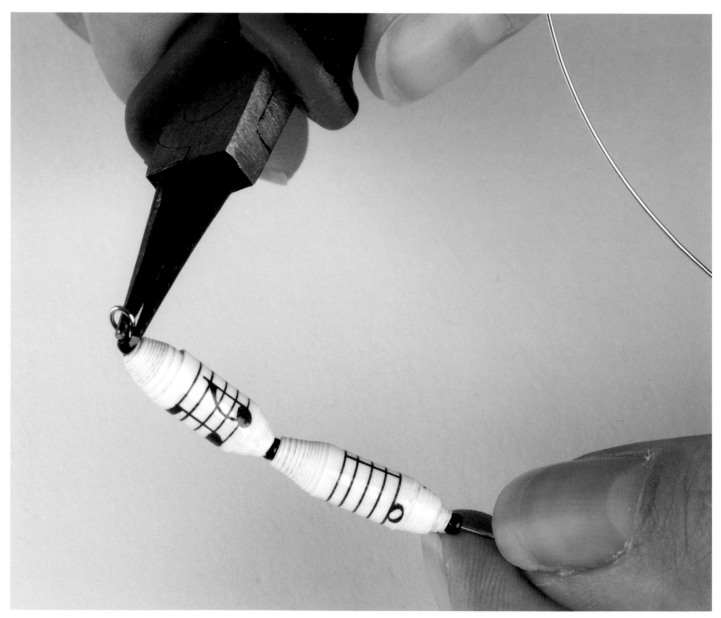

SCOTTIE DOG NOTE-HOLDER

A small note-holder is an ideal way to make a present of notelets, a voucher or a gift card. The Scottie dog motif has wide appeal and the green checked paper complements the black dogs. The circle ties for the string allow the folder to be used many times, making it a gift in itself.

1 ▽ Using the template on p. 120, cut the folder shape from the coral-coloured card. Score where indicated and crease the edges. Cut a rectangle of green checked paper measuring 11 x 15.5 cm [4¼ x 6⅛ in] and attach to the inside of the folder base.

You will need

- Basic tool kit
- Punches: Scottie dog 2.5 cm [1 in], circle punch 2.5 cm [1 in]
- Black paper, 5 x 7.5 cm [2 x 3 in]
- Coral card, 30 cm [11¾ in] square
- Black brads
- Memory wire, 45cm [18in]
- Green checked paper, 30 cm [11¾ in] square
- Cream notepaper, A4, 4 sheets

The dogs could be replaced by the punched flowers made in the gift tag project on p. 28.

2 ▷ Cut a strip of the green paper 3 cm [1¼ in] wide and 30 cm [12 in] long. Place this across the larger flap of the folder and attach so the edges wrap around the back. Then cut a strip measuring 3 x 15 cm [1¼ x 6 in] and attach on the inside of the flap.

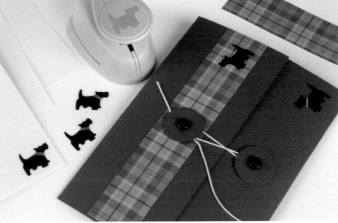

3 △ Using the circle punch, cut two circles from the remaining coral card, then make a hole in the centre of each with the needle tool. Pierce a central hole in the folder flap through the green checked paper at 8 cm [3⅛ in] from the edge. Insert the brad through the circle and the green paper. Spread the wings of the brad out on the reverse side. Repeat for the flap on the other side. Wrap the thin string around the circles.

4 △ Punch dog shapes from black card and embellish the strip of green checked paper with them. Fold the cream paper in half and then half again for notelets. Glue a punched dog shape to the corner. Here some of the dogs are decorated with thin collars of green paper, but this is optional.

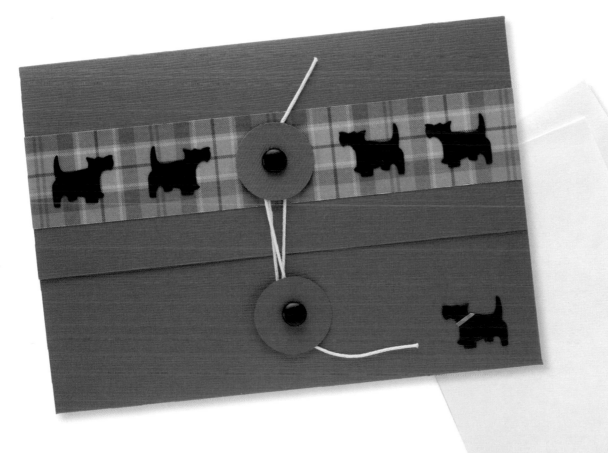

QUILLED PICTURE

This project uses paper quilling to create a pattern of pretty-coloured paper, showing the versatility of the craft. Contemporary colours bring this ancient technique bang up to date. The red and pink flowers use the technique illustrated on p. 26 for the butterfly wings, turning wings into petals instead. For the sprigs of green leaves the coiling and pinching technique of quilling is used, an ideal introduction for beginners to this craft. Finally the open swirls are filled in around the flowers and leaves for a finishing touch. This would make a great wedding or anniversary present. Letters and numbers can also be quilled if you want to personalize this picture. Note: do not place paper quilling in direct sunlight or it will fade.

You will need

- Basic tool kit
- Quilling papers, 3 mm [⅛ in] wide: red, pink, green, turquoise, light blue, light green
- Quilling tool
- Cream card, 19 cm [7½ in] square
- Wooden dowels, 1.5 cm [⅝ in] and 1 cm [⅜ in] diameter
- Picture frame, 25 cm [10 in] square, measuring outer edge

1 Start the larger flowers by wrapping a 15 cm [6 in] length of pink paper around the larger wooden dowel. Glue the end in place and slide the paper off the dowel, leaving a paper ring. Eight of these petals are needed for each of the three large pink flowers. Insert the end of a 10 cm [4 in] length of red paper into a quilling tool, coil tightly and glue the end in place for a tight coil – this is the centre of the flower. The four small red flowers are made in the same way, but with a 9 cm [3½ in] length of red wrapped around the smaller dowel. The centres of the red flowers are 5 cm [2 in] lengths of pink paper made into tight coils. Glue the flowers to the card.

2 ◁ Fold a 40 cm [15¾ in] length of red paper in half to find the centre. Insert one end in to the quilling tool to coil towards the centre. Remove the tool and coil the other end down to the centre. Remove the tool and a heart shape is made. Glue to the centre of the cream card.

3 ▷ To make the leaves, coil a 20 cm [7¾ in] length of green paper with the quilling tool. Remove the tool, let the coil unwind a little and glue the end in place. The sizes of the coils will vary, but this is fine as different sizes of leaves are needed.

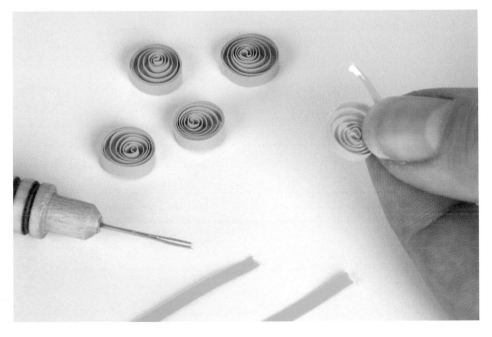

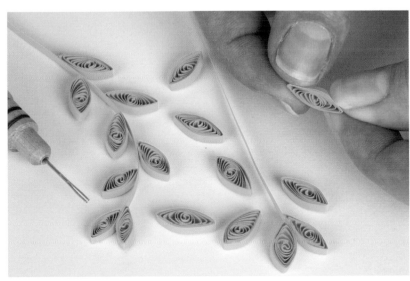

4 ◁ With your fingertips, lightly pinch each end of the coil to create two points, giving a leaf shape. Make eight leaves and glue them to an 8 cm [3⅛ in] length of green paper, which is the stalk. Repeat to make five more sprigs.

5 △ Now glue the six leaf sprigs on to the cream card, overlapping the flowers in some places to prevent the design from being too flat.

6 ▽ Using 20 cm [8 in] lengths of blue, green and turquoise paper, make long swirls, using the needle tool to curl each end to create an S shape. Pull out the ends slightly to unwind the coil a little, making it more open. Glue the swirls to the cream card. Mount the finished image inside a picture frame.

This picture project is quite time-consuming, but you can do it a little at a time. You can also make just a flower, leaves and a few swirls to make a greeting card.

POSY OF POPPIES

Paper flowers are a bright way of adding colour to your home all year round – especially poppies, which are bright and cheery. As real poppies don't last long once picked they don't feature in florists' arrangements, but by making your own you can have realistic paper flowers as a display. Crêpe paper is used for the petals as it is easy to cut and has some texture to it. The additional benefit of crepe paper is that it stretches, so when constructing the flower it moulds and allows more handling.

You will need

- Basic tool kit
- Crêpe paper in red and black, a pack of each
- Floristry wire, 18 gauge, five 25 cm [10 in] lengths
- Green paper floristry tape
- Sponge
- Circle punch, 1.5 cm [⅝ in]
- Silver 3D paint
- Black tissue paper, one pack

1 ▷ Cut a clean sponge into five 1 cm [⅜ in] squares. Place one on each length of wire and bend the end of the wire over to secure the sponge. Punch circles of card 1.5 cm [⅝ in] in diameter and glue one to each sponge. (Scrap card can be used for these.)

2 ◁ Cover one of the sponge heads with a circle of black crêpe paper 8 cm [3⅛ in] in diameter and wrap the crêpe around the wire. Use the green floristry tape to secure the crêpe paper – as the tape is sticky it adheres to itself. Repeat this for all five poppy heads.

3 ▷ Using silver 3D paint, draw lines on the poppy head, following the circle of the card underneath as a guide to the size. Leave to dry fully before moving on to the next step.

If you don't have silver 3D paint for the flowers you can use silver pen to draw on the crêpe. Alternatively, cut strips of silver card and glue them on.

4 ▽ Cut a piece of black tissue paper measuring 10 x 20 cm [4 x 7¾ in] and fold over lengthways. With large scissors, cut across the fold for 2 cm [¾ in]. Move the scissors along 2 mm [¹⁄₁₆ in] and cut again, then continue in this way to fringe the paper. Repeat for each poppy.

5 △ Wrap a piece of the black tissue paper around each poppy head, fringed edges uppermost. Attach the bottom, unfringed edge around the wire with green tape.

6 ▽ Each poppy has seven red petals. Copy the petal template from p. 124 and cut around this on red crêpe paper – several layers can be cut at the same time to speed up the process. Position three petals around each flower centre and tape in place, then position another four and tape again.

STENCILLED PENCIL POT AND NOTE-HOLDER

Stencilling is the method of colouring through a template to leave a design once the template is removed. There are many stencils available to purchase, but with some straightforward paper cutting you can make your own unique designs and by moving the stencil over a sheet of paper you can quickly build up a pattern. In this project, two leaf-shaped stencils are used with three colours. A tin from the kitchen cupboard is cleaned and covered with the stencilled paper to make a pencil holder or desk tidy.

You will need

- Basic tool kit
- Scrap card
- Green card, 7.5 x 27 cm [3 x 10⅝ in]
- Ink pads: green, purple, red
- Sponge
- Tin, 8 cm [3⅛ in] diameter and 8 cm [3⅛ in] high

You can use punches or die-cutters to make shapes in card for stencils.

1 ◁ Copy the two leaf templates from p. 127 and tape on to scrap card. Using a small knife, cut out the patterns following the templates, cutting through the paper and card at the same time.

2 ▷ Place the green card on scrap paper. Take the larger leaf stencil and place it on the green card. Dab the piece of clean sponge on to the purple ink pad to pick up ink, then press the sponge through the stencil on to the green card. Continue to colour in, using this method until the leaf shapes are all purple. Remove the stencil and reposition above the first pattern, then sponge again. Once that is complete move the stencil along and with another piece of sponge and a pink ink pad, colour in pink leaves.

3 △ Continue sponging in this way all along the green strip of card. Then change to the other leaf stencil and with a clean sponge and green ink, add green leaves.

4 ▽ Once the green card is fully stencilled, leave to dry for a few minutes. Place double-sided tape on the reverse side, all along the four edges, then wrap the card round the tin.

Variation Note-holder

This technique can also be adapted to make a matching note-holder.

FOLDED PAPER PICTURE

Paper folding is a historic craft, but in Holland in the 1990s Tiny van der Plas developed a new form when she folded teabag envelopes then slotted them together to form rosettes. Since then the idea of arranging identically folded squares of paper has become popular for the ease of folding and stylish results. The ethos of recycling paper has been used here with two old maps cut up and folded for a picture. It is often hard to craft gifts for men, but they will appreciate the technical papercrafts here!

You will need

- Basic tool kit
- Old maps
- Picture frame, 16.5 cm [6½ in] square, measuring outer edge
- Green card, 14.5 cm [5¾ in] square

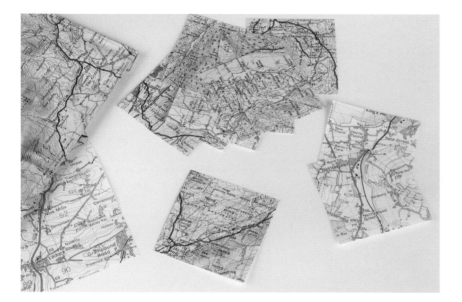

1 △ Here two maps are used for light and dark squares. Cut the maps into strips, choosing interesting areas, and then cut 5 cm [2 in] squares of each.

For a quicker version of this project it could be adapted in to a gift tag or greetings card by arranging the folded shapes in to a rosette. This requires 8 folded pieces.

2 ◁ Take one square of paper and fold edge to edge with the pattern innermost. Crease along the edge with your fingers.

3 ▷ Open the square of paper out, and with the pattern outermost fold over corner to corner and crease. Open the paper out and fold the other corner to corner, then open slightly, so you have three crease lines.

4 ▽ Push the sides of the square inwards to form a hat or triangle shape. I find it easiest to start a production line and get all squares to this stage before moving on.

5 ▷ Each shape has four corners. Take one corner and fold it under, towards the point of the triangle. Take the other corner of the same side and fold it under in the same way, to the point. You now have a triangle shape but with a folded square on the front. Fold all the pieces in this way.

6 ◁ Each triangle now has only two corners. Take one corner and fold upwards away from the point of the triangle. Take the other corner and fold it up in the same way. Now both of these two corners are together and pointing away from the folded square.

7 ◁ Once all the pieces have been folded in this way, take four of the darker colour and position together in the centre of the green card, so that each folded square is together. Glue in place. Take one of the lighter colour, tuck under the edge of the darker piece and glue.

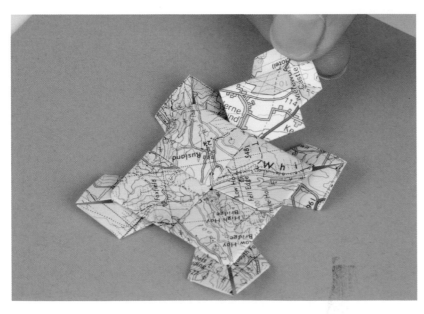

8 ▷ Continue to build up the design by tucking under and glueing the lighter pieces to form a cross shape. Then fill in with light and dark pieces as shown. Mount the finished image inside a picture frame.

Holidays and special occasions

All over the world, paper has long been used to make decorations for holidays and ceremonies of many kinds. Not only is it widely available in many types suitable for decorations such as tissue, crêpe and mulberry, paper is a creative material that is easy to use. Tissue pompoms and paper quilling are examples of this, where flamboyant ornamentations are made from standard paper and tissue. Seasonal festivities can involve the whole family in making garlands and wreaths, using colours that reflect the current trends to keep decorations fresh and special. Make interiors elegant with baby garlands, table settings and accessories or Halloween displays that are stylish and original, delighting your guests.

CHRISTMAS GARLANDS

Garlands play a major role in decorations for holidays and celebrations. Here concertina stars are strung on to organza ribbon for a decorative garland. The two sizes of concertina star are layered for extra effect, but a single concertina layer would be equally as effective. Reds and greens are used for the festive season, but the garlands could be adapted to red and blue for a patriotic event or pinks and blues for a baby shower.

You will need

- Basic tool kit
- Red and green patterned papers, 29 cm [11½ in] lengths
- Small star punch
- Circle punch, 1.5 cm [⅝ in]
- Cream card, 10 x 13 cm [4 x 5 in]

These concertinas can be scaled up to larger sizes by doubling the length and widths.

1 ◁ Take a red patterned paper strip 29 cm [11½ in] long by 3.5 cm [1⅜ in] wide and concertina fold at every 4 cm [1½ in] to the end.

2 ▷ With large scissors, cut through all the layers from the folded edges up to the open section to create a point.

3 ▷ Open out the strip, then fold and concertina the length, spacing each fold at 6mm [¼ in] all the way along. It does not matter if the folds vary in size slightly – it is more important to keep the same number of folds in each section. Glue the ends of the paper together.

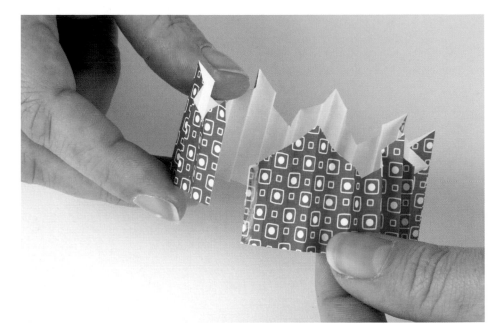

4 ▽ Using the punch, make a circle of card, spread glue on the card, then flatten the concertina circle to the glue, holding it in place as it dries or it will spring up. Repeat steps 1–4 with a green paper strip 29 cm [11½ in] long by 2.5 cm [1 in] wide.

5 △ Glue the smaller concertina star on top of the larger star. Use a small star punch to make a star from red paper and glue to the top concertina. Continue to make more concertinas, alternating the colours for the larger and smaller layers.

6 ▽ Make a hole in the point of one large concertina star and thread narrow organza ribbon through. Tie a loose knot then thread the next star on the ribbon. Continue threading and tying concertina stars on for the length you require. You can space them wider apart than is shown here if you wish.

FRINGED FRILLY FLOWER PICTURE

Bright flowers are always a welcome sight, cheerful and eye-catching. These flowers are made from gift wrap that has been cut and fringed. Lengths of pink and yellow paper are joined together then the whole length is coiled tightly. The result, when opened out, is a pretty flower with long, straight petals. With three grouped together the flowers make a great picture, but they could also be adapted for a wedding theme, decorating place names, menus and napkin rings.

You will need

- Basic tool kit
- A roll of striped gift wrap
- Quilling tool
- Pink and yellow paper, 10mm [⅜ in] wide)
- Picture frame, 25 cm [10 in] square, measuring outer edge

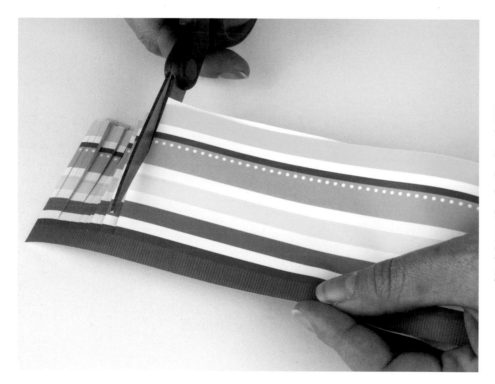

1 ◁ Cut a piece of paper 40 cm [15¾ in] long by 7 cm [2¾ in] wide, with the stripes running along the length. Using scissors, cut across the paper, but not the whole way across, leaving an uncut margin of about 6 mm [¼ in]. Repeat along the whole length, leaving a 2 mm [¹⁄₁₆ in] gap between cuts.

Gift wrap is a good weight of paper for these flowers, but you can also experiment with other types of paper such as old books or music sheets. If the sheet of paper is not long enough you can glue two lengths together.

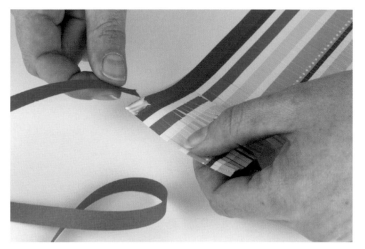

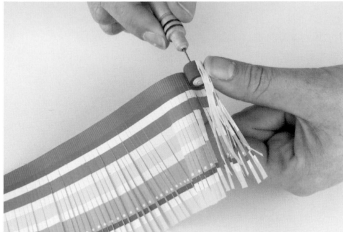

2 △ Glue a 40 cm [15¾ in] length of the pink paper to the uncut margin at one end, and then glue a 20 cm [7¾ in] length of the yellow paper to the pink length.

3 △ Insert the end of the yellow paper into the slot of the quilling tool and coil by turning the quilling tool and keeping tension on the paper with the other hand.

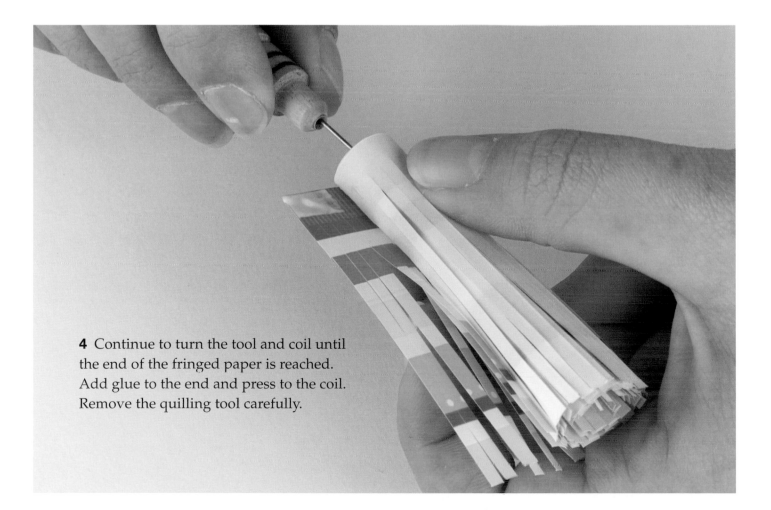

4 Continue to turn the tool and coil until the end of the fringed paper is reached. Add glue to the end and press to the coil. Remove the quilling tool carefully.

5 ▷ Now put your finger into the flower centre and press down. The fringed pieces will splay outwards, revealing the yellow and pink centre to the flower.

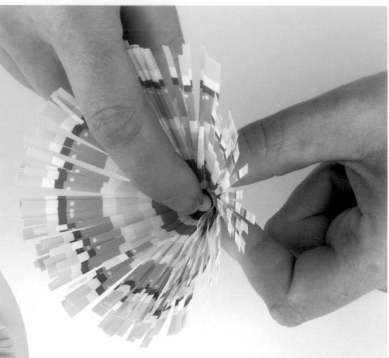

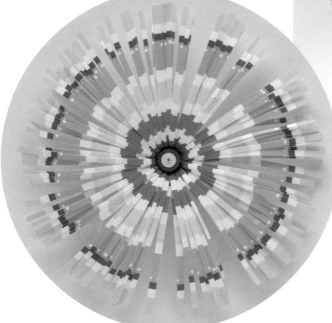

6 ▽ Make two more fringed flowers in this way, using different sections of the striped pattern of the gift wrap. For the first flower cut the paper 40 x 6 cm [15¾ x 2⅜ in] and 40 x 4.5 cm [15¾ x 1¾ in] for the smaller flower. Glue to a square of cream card and insert into the frame.

BABY BUNTING

Baby showers or celebrations are a time to pull out the stops and create something special. Here bunting is made by stitching triangles of card on to ribbon for draping across a door or entrance. Cute prams decorate each triangle and scalloped edges add frills and style. The die-cutting machine needed for this project was once a luxury item to crafters but has become an essential part of the tool kit for many serious crafters now. It is a pricey investment, but the advantage it offers is the huge variety of die cuts now available, which make professional shapes such as the scallop circles used here. Use the template on p. 122 for the main triangle the size can be altered depending on how big or small you want your bunting.

You will need

- Basic tool kit
- Blue card, two sheets 30.5 cm [12 in] square
- Paper (any types): shades of blue and cream, 10 cm square for each colour
- Patterned buttons
- Scallop-edge scissors
- Die cut machine and scalloped circle die, 6 cm [2⅜ in] diameter
- Needle and blue thread
- Ribbon, 1.6 m [5ft 3 in]
- Light blue felt pen
- Strong glue

1 Using the die cut machine and scalloped circle die, cut out circles from four shades of blue paper.

2 ◁ Take one scalloped circle and cut out a quarter segment. Put the segment aside for step 3. On the remaining circle, using a blue pen, draw lines on the adjacent quarter, radiating from the centre to the edge.

3 ▽ With small scissors, cut a handle from the separated quarter, using the rounded scallop edge as the curved handle bar, then cutting straight for the side of the handle. Glue to the three-quarter scallop circle as shown.

The colour scheme can be changed to pink for a girl. Alternatively, a rainbow colour scheme would look fabulous and avoid the usual gender-defining colours.

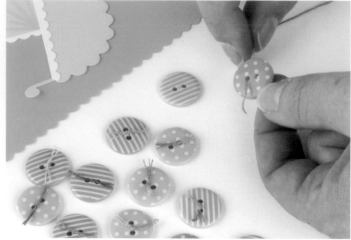

4 △ Take a length of cream paper and, with scallop-edge scissors, cut along it to make a scalloped edge. Now cut a straight line along underneath this to leave a narrow strip that is scalloped only on one side. Attach a length across the pram shape and a strip on the pram hood as a trim.

5 △ Thread the patterned buttons with blue thread, tie a knot and trim the ends. Attach the pram shape to a triangle of card with scallop edges, cut with scissors. Use strong glue to attach buttons to the card.

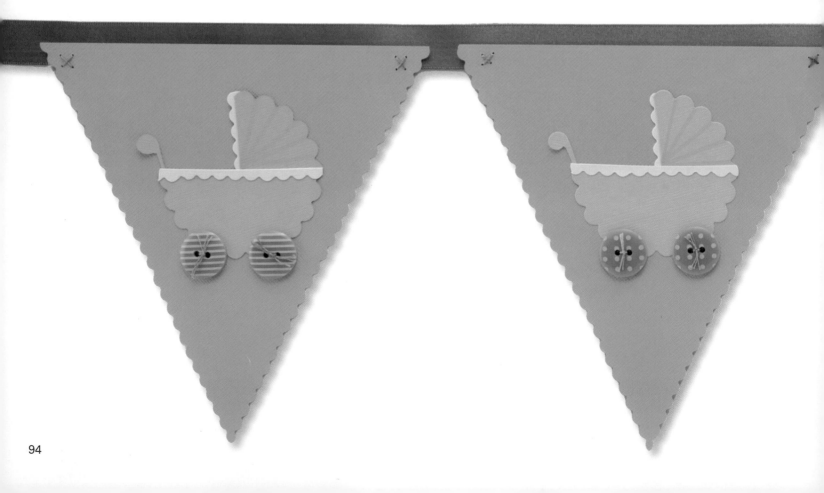

6 ▽ Thread a needle with blue thread. Prick four holes in one top corner of the card triangle and then stitch the card to the length of blue ribbon, tying the thread on the reverse side. Stitch the other corner of the triangle to the ribbon and continue adding more triangles.

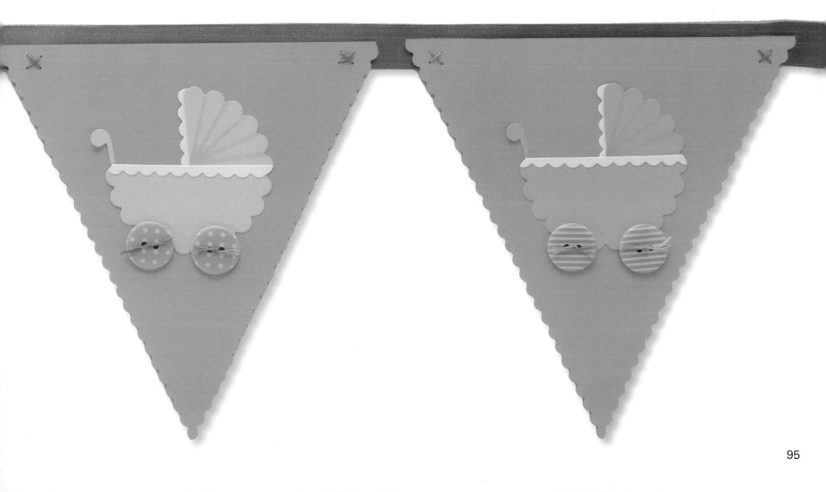

LEOPARD-PRINT STYLE

Animal print never goes out of style and fashionistas will adore these leopard-print shoes and handbag. Simply by colouring plain paper or card you can transform it into a fabulous design that will be loved by teenagers and those a little further on in years! The shoe card can be personalized, perhaps with a price tag with the recipient's age on or a greeting. These would be ideal for hen party/bachelorette party invites.

Animal prints don't have to be brown – you can really jazz up these items by using pink card with pink and black pens.

You will need

- Basic tool kit
- Card: brown 15 x 30 cm
- light brown 15 x 30 cm
- Felt pens: dark brown, light brown, black
- Clear gemstones
- Black ribbon 1 cm wide by 20 cm long
- Circle punch 1.5 cm diameter

1 Using the template on p. 122, cut out two shoe shapes from light brown card.

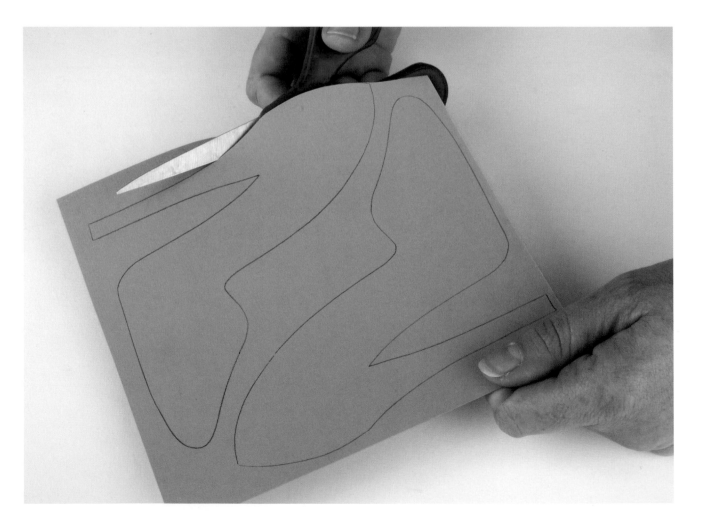

2 △ Place the shoes on scrap paper and colour the heels dark brown, using the felt pen. Then draw a line along the sole and the inner edge of the shoe with dark brown pen. With the light brown pen, roughly colour shapes on the shoe. These need to be random and variable in size.

3 ▽ With the black pen, colour the edge of each shape, but do not completely enclose them. Attach three clear gemstones to each shoe toe. Make two ribbon shapes from card and colour them black, then attach them to the top of the heels.

4 △ Now join the two shoe shapes together with a piece of card 10 cm [4 in] long by 2 cm [¾ in] wide, folded into three to form a zigzag. Attach one end to the reverse side of one shoe, and then repeat with the other shoe. Before the glue dries ensure the shoes stand up and fold flat. If not, wiggle the joining card until they do.

5 ▽ Cut out a handbag shape and handbag flap from brown card (see template p. 121). Using the same pens and method, colour in the animal print on the card. Colour a line along the handbag flap with brown pen. Attach the handbag flap over the top of the front of the bag, then glue on black ribbon for the handle. Use a circle punch to make a circle from the brown card, colour it black and add a gemstone. Attach to the bag.

POMPOM TISSUE-FLOWER HEART

Pompom flowers made from tissue have a long history and probably originated in Mexico as part of celebrations where folk art was used to create colourful displays. The tissue paper was, and still is, a cheaper alternative to real flowers and can easily make a large, bright display that will last a lot longer than flowers as well! After concertina-folding layers of tissue, then binding them in the middle, you can fluff up the layers to make the flower three-dimensional. In these examples two colours of tissue are used to add more vibrancy. These could make a dazzling display at a wedding or anniversary event.

You will need

- Basic tool kit
- Packs of tissue paper, pink and light pin
- Cream or light pink mount board, 30.5 cm [12 in] square
- Pink embroidery thread

Don't worry if you tear the tissue a little, as the tear becomes part of the flower and is not noticeable. Rather than rounding the ends, you can also experiment with cutting them to points. Very large pompom flowers can be made with a whole sheet of tissue paper.

1 △ Start by layering six sheets of dark pink and two sheets of light pink, measuring 25 x 11 cm [10 x 4¼ in]. Then fold over at 2 cm [¾ in] along the short edge. Turn over, fold again at 2 cm [¾ in] and continue to fold to concertina the whole tissue, keeping the layers together.

2 △ At the middle of the length, tie a thread measuring 20 cm [7¾ in] around the folded tissue. Tie this quite tightly and secure with a double knot so it will not slip. Trim the excess thread.

3 ▷ With scissors, cut the ends of the folded tissue into a curve. Cutting through the layers requires a fair amount of pressure, so larger scissors are best for this.

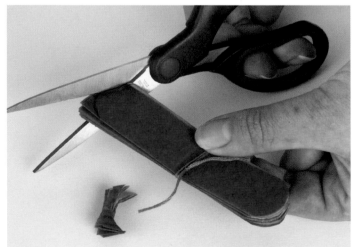

4 ◁ With the dark pink tissue uppermost, lift the top layer of tissue upwards, away from the layers underneath. It takes practice to determine the force needed to pull upwards without tearing the tissue all the way through. Continue to pull the layers upwards and separate them as much as possible. The light pink tissue will now be at the base of the flower.

5 ▷ Make six tissue pompoms in this way. For a second batch of six, at step 4 start fluffing up with the light pink tissue uppermost, then the light pink tissue becomes the centre. Twelve pompoms are needed in total for this project. Cut the heart shape from strong card, using the template on p. 126. Alternate the dark and light pink flowers and glue to the heart shape.

WOVEN STAR CHRISTMAS DECORATIONS

Woven stars have been a traditional Scandinavian holiday decoration for many years and can be brought up-to-date with modern patterned papers, not only for Christmas decorations but also for parties or other celebrations. Double-sided card is used for the project as both sides are visible, to make them ideal for hanging where they are viewed from all sides. If you don't have card that is patterned on both sides you can make your own colouring with pens or glue a thin sheet of paper to the back with spray adhesive.

You will need

- Basic tool kit
- Card or thick paper with a pattern or colour on each side, a sheet of 30.5 cm [12 in] square will make one star
- Zigzag-edge scissors
- Ribbon
- Wooden dowel, 2.5 cm [1 in] diameter

1 Cut eight strips of card measuring 1 x 30 cm [⅜ x 12 in]. Then cut two strips measuring 2 x 30 cm [¾ x 12 in].

2 ◁ With the zigzag-edge scissors, cut the edges of the 2 cm [¾ in] wide strips on both sides, then cut them in half to make four lengths of 15 cm [6 in].

3 ▽ Take two zigzag strips and glue them together to form a cross shape. Attach two long strips of card each side of the vertical zigzag piece. Then weave two more long strips across to form a grid. Make two of these.

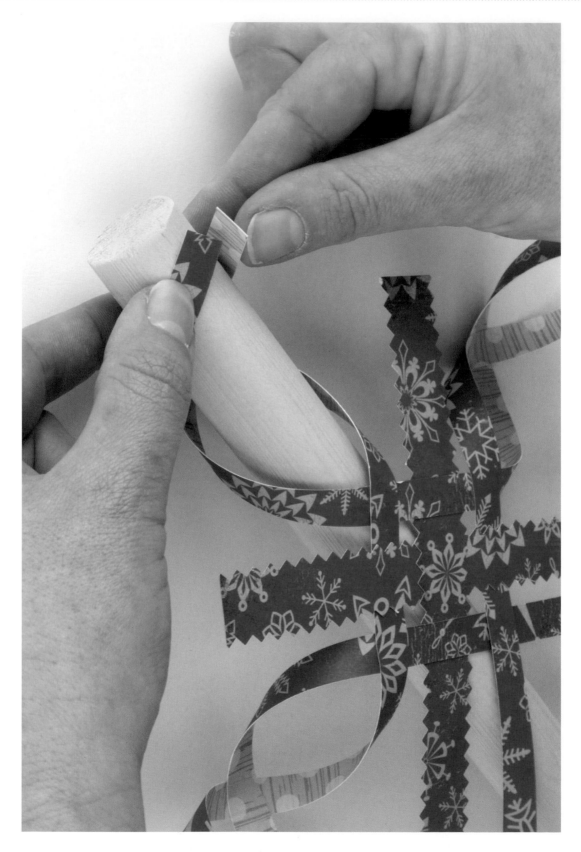

4 From the corner of one grid, take two ends down and round the wooden dowel and then back up. Glue the tips together to create a loop shape. Glue where the lengths cross each other under the dowel. Repeat this three more times at each corner. Repeat with the other woven grid.

If you prefer you can use a crafter's guillotine to cut the card strips.

5 Turn one shape over and place over the top of the first shape, lining them up so the looped shapes are on top of the middle horizontal and vertical strips. Slot the ends of the short zigzag lengths into the loops.

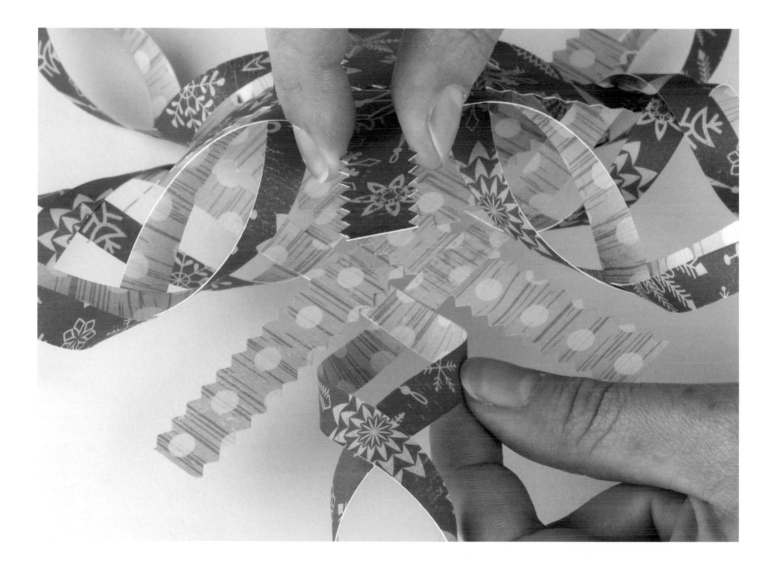

5 Glue the ends in place so the star holds its shape. Make a hole in one point and thread ribbon through if you wish.

HALLOWEEN DECORATION

Spiders and cobwebs are an essential part of any Halloween celebration, and the spookier the better. This window decoration or display uses two techniques of paper cutting for the web and quilling for the spiders. The intricate cutting of the web requires some attention, but the result is effective. With the quilled spiders the added dimension the paper gives makes them more realistic – good for some people, but not for arachnaphobes!

1 Copy the cobweb design on p. 123 on to a piece of orange card measuring 26 x 30.5 cm [10¼ x 12 in]. Place on a cutting mat. With a craft knife, cut out the inner shapes, leaving only the threads and spokes of the web.

You will need

- Basic tool kit
- Card: orange and black, 30.5 cm [12 in] square
- Parchment paper, 28 x 33 cm [11 x 13 in]
- Quilling paper: black and green with metallic green edge, 3 mm [⅛ in] wide
- Quilling tool
- Picture frame 30 cm [12 in] wide by 35 cm [13⅕ in] long outermost edges

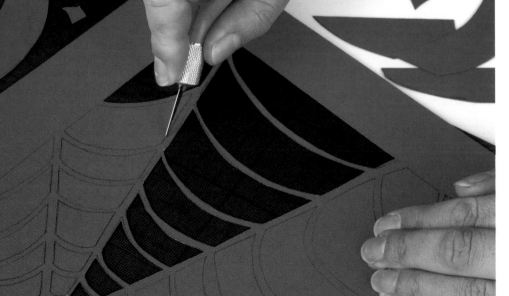

It is essential to put a new blade in a craft knife when cutting a design as large as this to ensure clean and easy cutting. The quilling may be tricky for a beginner, but ready-made plastic spiders can be used instead.

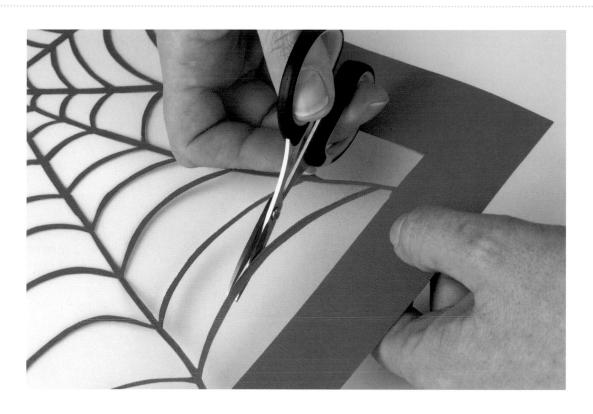

2 △ If you slip through a section do not worry as this is part of the design – if you don't, snip a couple of sections at the end for cobweb authenticity. Use small scissors to tidy up some of the inner web so the threads are even and neat.

3 ▽ Now attach the sheet of parchment paper to the reverse side of the orange cobweb, then a frame of black card on the top front of the orange card. To make the frame cut two strips of the black card 2.5 x 27.5 cm [1 x 11 in] and two more strips 2.5 x 30.5 cm [1 x 12 in]. Glue together.

4 ◁ For the quilled spiders, start by making a head from three 40 cm [15¾ in] lengths of black quilling paper, glued end to end to make one 1.2 m [4 ft] length. Insert one end into the quilling tool, coil tightly and glue the end in place. Then, with your thumb, push up the inner part of the coil to make a dome and glue the inside. Leave to dry. Make two smaller domes, using only two 40 cm [15¾ in] lengths each.

5 ▽ For the quilled spider body, use three lengths of green with metallic green edge, glued end to end, and one length of black paper glued to one end, making a length of 1.6 m [5 ft 3 in]. With the quilling tool, make a loose closed coil and glue the end in place. Make another two bodies, each with two green and one black lengths.

6 ▷ Cut four 10 cm [4 in] lengths of black paper and attach to the large body, then attach the large head. For the smaller spiders, the legs are 7 cm [2¾ in] long. Glue to the cobweb and insert into a black picture frame. You can add googly eyes if you wish to make the spiders more friendly.

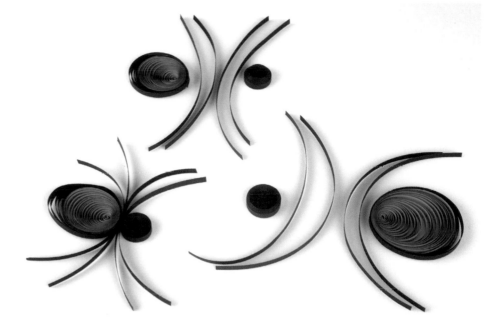

CHRISTMAS POINSETTIA WREATH

Poinsettia flowers are a staple of festive decorations for many nowadays. Here the bright red flowers are switched to warm, muted browns for subtle petals and leaves. The stamped paper, which adds an interesting element, has been created by rubber stamping on to plain paper, but you could use preprinted designs if you lack a stamp or want to save time. These poinsettia flowers also look good when made from red and green patterned papers, so you may want to experiment if you already have those papers in your collection.

You will need

- Basic tool kit
- Cream paper two sheets 30 cm [12 in] square
- Brown card 15 x 30 cm [6 x 12 in]
- Cream mount board 23 cm [9 in] square
- Brown ink pad
- Rubber stamp for script and acrylic block
- Gold glitter
- Sponge
- Circle punch, small 1 cm diameter

1 Put the script stamp on to the acrylic block, ink the stamp with brown ink by dabbing the ink pad on to the stamp. Print on to cream paper. Then ink the stamp again and print again until you have covered the whole sheet with the printed design.

2 ◁ Using the template on p. 117, cut petals from the printed sheet – five large and four or five small for each of the six flowers. Take half the large and half the small petals one at a time and run the edges over the brown ink pad to colour them. Put these aside. Place the remaining petals on scrap paper and colour the outer edges with a sponge dabbed in the brown ink.

3 ▽ Once the ink is dry, bend the petals and shape them with your hands.

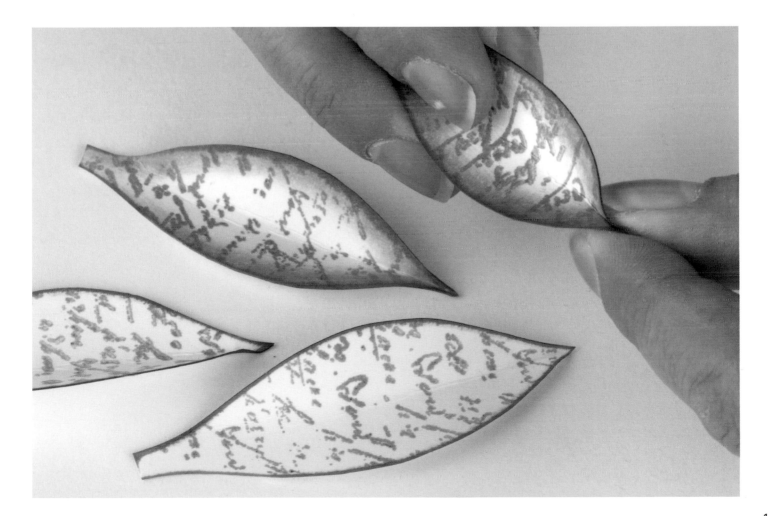

4 ▷ Punch a small circle from cream paper and glue five large petals to the circle. Make sure the petals are spaced to look like a star shape. Then glue four or five smaller petals on top. Use the same petals, dark or light, per flower. Repeat with the remaining flowers.

5 ◁ Add dabs of gold glitter to the centre of each flower and to the very tips of the light-coloured flowers. Leave to dry.

6 ▷ Cut leaf shapes from brown card, using the large poinsettia petal template as a guide. Bend the leaves. Cut a circle of mount board 22 cm [8½ in] in diameter and cut the inner circle 16 cm [6¼ in]. Glue six flowers in total to the circle and add as many leaves as necessary to make a wreath.

TEMPLATES FOR ENLARGEMENT

These templates are not actual size, measurements used for projects featured have been noted for reference purposes. Templates can be photocopied and scaled to your preference for your project.

New-Home Pop Up Card
page 40

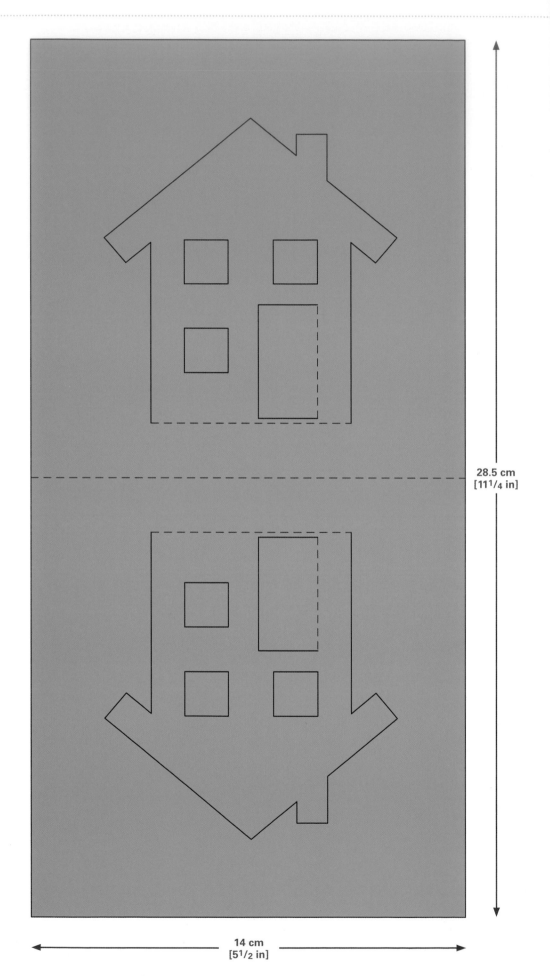

28.5 cm
[11¹/₄ in]

14 cm
[5¹/₂ in]

Kirigami Card
page 42

Christmas Poinsettia Wreath
page 112

Note Block with Roses
page 56

Large Rose

Owl Gift Tags
page 32

Small Rose

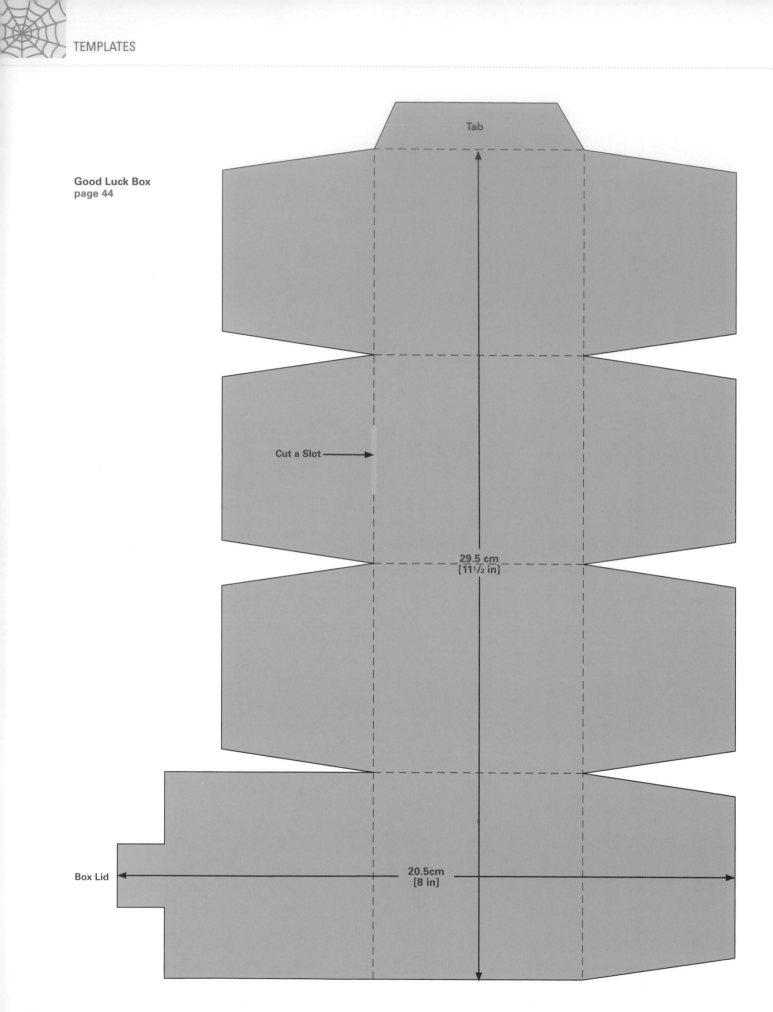

Good Luck Box
page 44

Tab

Cut a Slot ——→

29.5 cm
[11½ in]

Box Lid

20.5cm
[8 in]

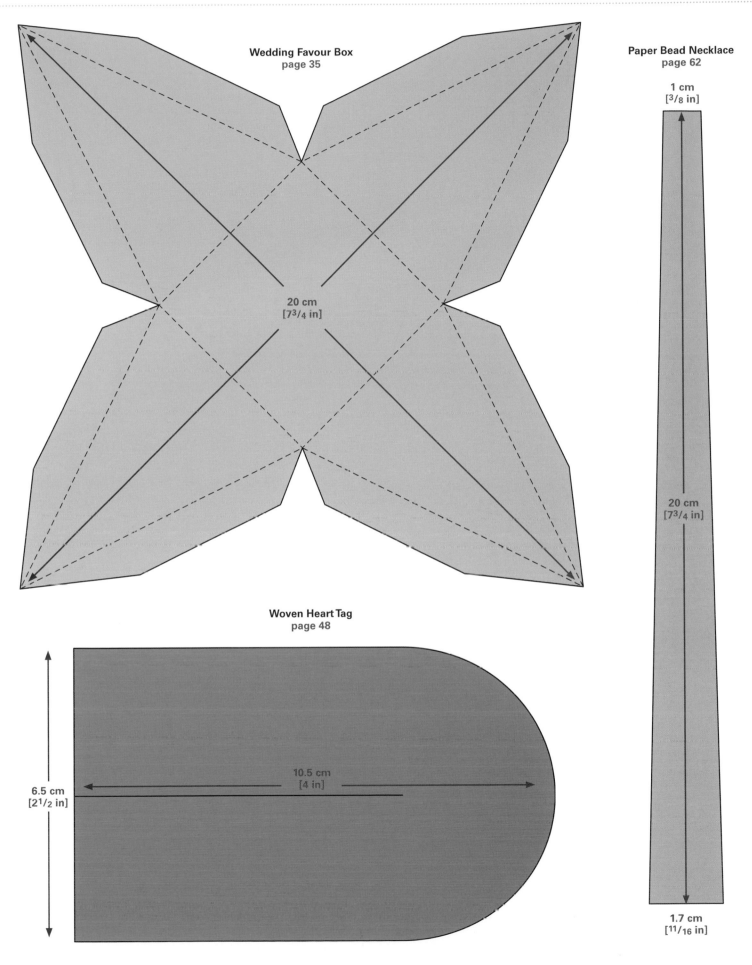

Wedding Favour Box
page 35

Paper Bead Necklace
page 62

1 cm
[3/8 in]

20 cm
[7³/4 in]

20 cm
[7³/4 in]

1.7 cm
[11/16 in]

Woven Heart Tag
page 48

6.5 cm
[2¹/2 in]

10.5 cm
[4 in]

119

Scottie Dog Note-Holder
page 66

25 cm
[10 in]

20cm
[7³/4 in]

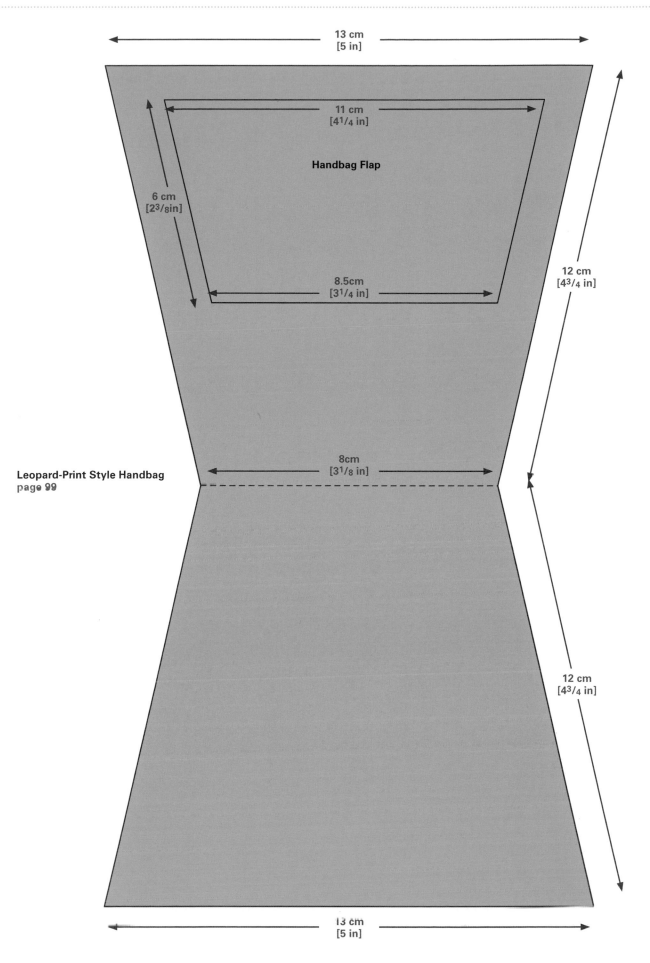

13 cm
[5 in]

11 cm
[4¹/₄ in]

Handbag Flap

6 cm
[2³/₈in]

8.5cm
[3¹/₄ in]

12 cm
[4³/₄ in]

8cm
[3¹/₈ in]

Leopard-Print Style Handbag
page 99

12 cm
[4³/₄ in]

13 cm
[5 in]

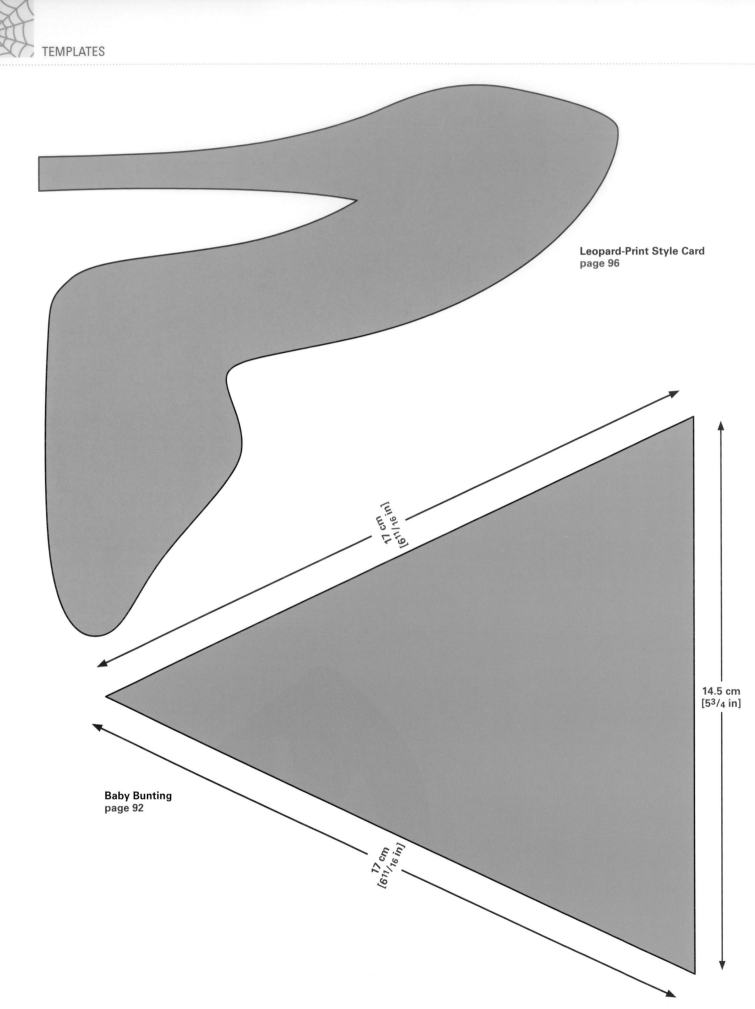

Leopard-Print Style Card
page 96

17 cm
[6¹¹/₁₆ in]

14.5 cm
[5³/₄ in]

Baby Bunting
page 92

17 cm
[6¹¹/₁₆ in]

Halloween Decoration
page 108

TEMPLATES

Punched Tags
page 28

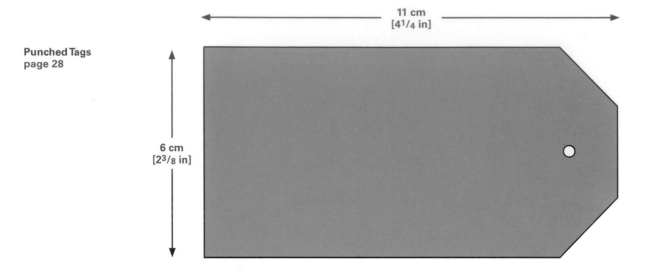

11 cm
[4¹/₄ in]

6 cm
[2³/₈ in]

Posy of Poppies
page 72

124

Rubber-Stamped Envelope
page 38

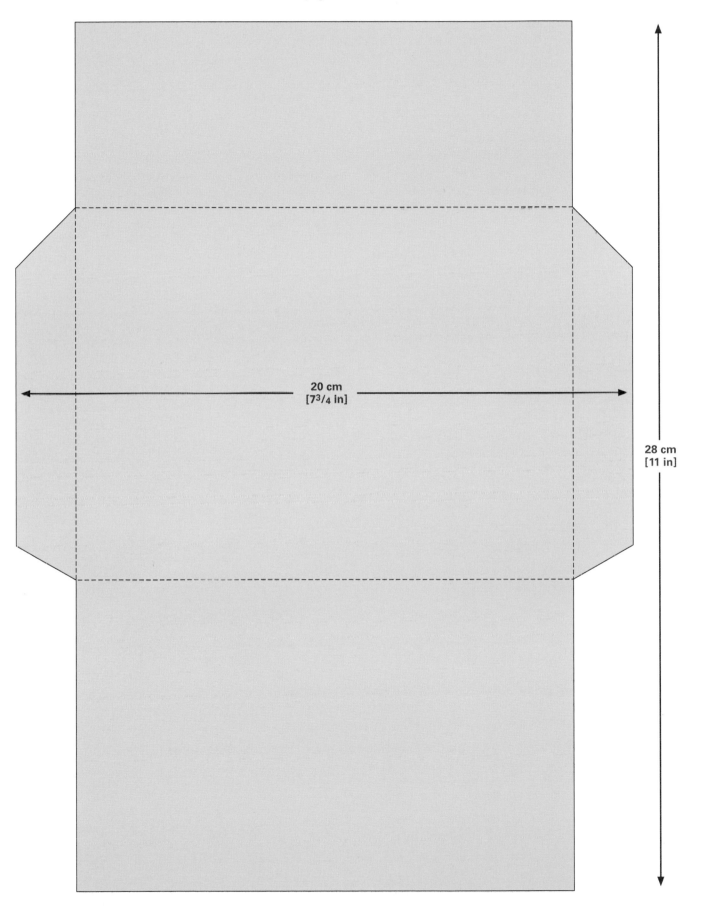

20 cm
[7³/₄ in]

28 cm
[11 in]

Pompom Tissue Flower Heart
page 100

27.5 cm
[11 in]

27.5 cm
[11 in]

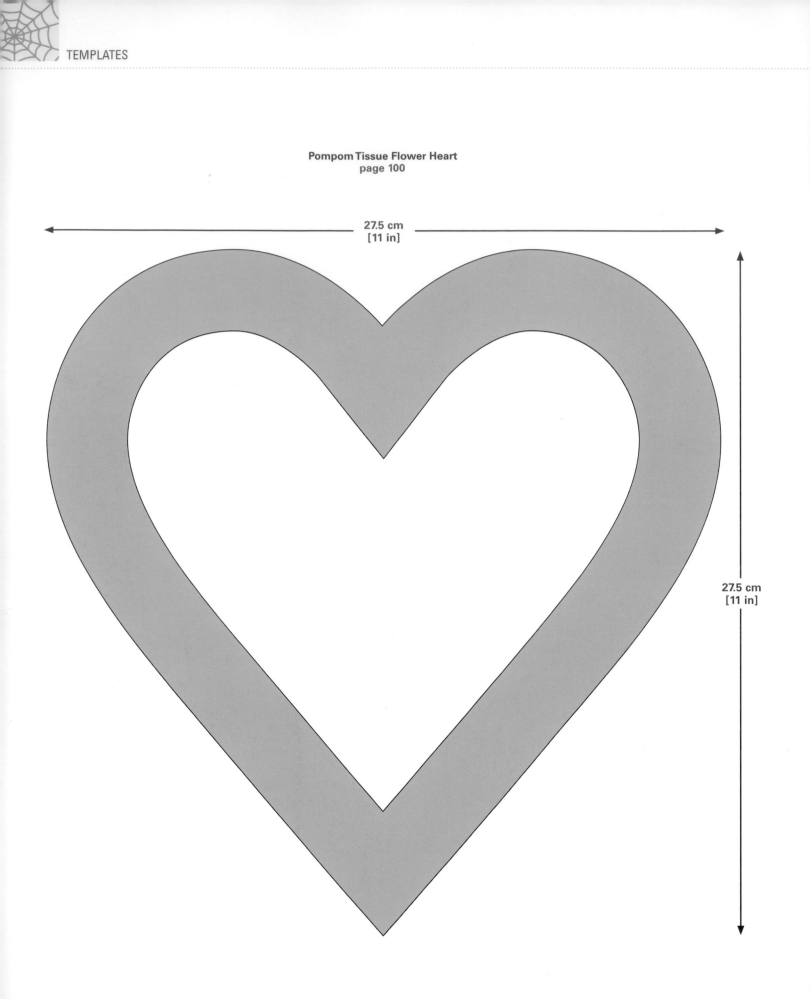

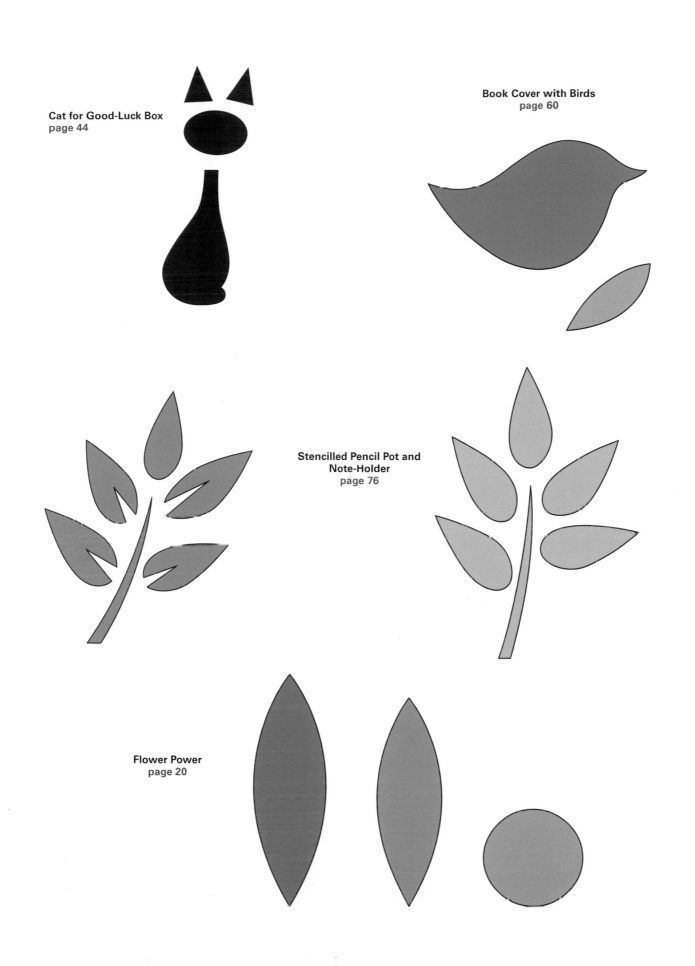

Cat for Good-Luck Box
page 44

Book Cover with Birds
page 60

Stencilled Pencil Pot and Note-Holder
page 76

Flower Power
page 20

ACKNOWLEDGEMENTS

I would like to thank the team at Arcturus Publishing for giving me the opportunity to indulge my passion for papercrafts in creating this fabulous book.

Many thanks to Karl Adamson for all the step photography, greatly helping to make everything clear and easy to follow.

Thank you to Diane Boden of JJ Quilling Design for the quality paper strips and tools used in the quilling projects. Many thanks to Sizzix for creating the wonderful Big Shot die cutting tool that allows us crafters to make fabulous papercrafts using the huge array of die cut templates. I would also like to thank Woodware for producing wonderful rubber stamps, punches and products that become part of a crafters toolkit. And finally thanks to Fiskars for great cutting tools and Letraset for professional pens, all essential in the making of this book.